MY GARDEN (BOOK):

MY GARDEN (BOOK):

JAMAICA KINCAID

ILLUSTRATIONS BY JILL FOX

Farrar Straus Giroux
New York

Farrar, Straus and Giroux

19 Union Square West, New York 10003

Distributed in Canada by Douglas & McIntyre Ltd.

Printed in the United States of America

Designed by Susan Mitchell

First edition, 1999

Library of Congress Cataloging-in-Publication Data

Kincaid, Jamaica.

My garden (book): / Jamaica Kincaid.

p.   cm.

ISBN 0-374-28186-6 (alk. paper)

1. Gardens—Anecdotes.   2. Gardening—Anecdotes.   3. Kincaid,

Jamaica.   4. Gardeners—Anecdotes.   I. Title.

SB455.K48   1999

635—dc21   99–26204

Some essays in this book have appeared, in slightly different form,

in *Architectural Digest*, *DoubleTake*, *The New Yorker*, and *Travel &

Leisure*.

With blind, instinctive, and confused love,
for Annie
&
for Harold
who from time to time are furiously certain
that the only thing standing between them and a
perfect union with their mother is the garden, and
from time to time, they are correct

CONTENTS

My Garden (Book):

I

MY GARDEN (BOOK):

$\mathcal{M}$y attachment in adult life to the garden begins in this way: shortly after I became a mother for the first time, my husband gave me a hoe, a rake, a spade, a fork, some flower seeds to mark the occasion of that thing known as Mother's Day. It was my second Mother's Day; for the first one he had given me a pair of earrings and I put them on a table in the kitchen and they were never seen again, by me, nor anyone else, not the lady who cleaned the house, not the women who helped me take care of my child, not my husband, not my child—no one admitted to ever seeing them again. I can't remember if the seeds and tools were wrapped up, but I can remember that immediately on having them I went outside and dug up a large part of the small yard, a patch that had never been cultivated, and put all the seeds in the packets in the ground.

And that was that, for nothing grew, the ground was improperly prepared, it was in the shade of a big oak tree and a big maple tree (those
two trees really did grow in the same vicinity and I did not appreciate
them then; so annoying, their leaves falling down in the autumn and
dirtying up the yard, I thought then).

A man named Chet lived in the house right next to me and he
could breathe properly only while attached to canisters filled with oxygen; then every once in a while he would come outside and smoke a
cigarette, and while smoking a cigarette he would tend to these enormous tomatoes that he grew right up against the side of his house. The
tomatoes were exposed fully to the sun in that position and he did not
worry about poisonous toxins leaching out of the materials from which
his house was built into the soil in which his tomatoes were grown.
His tomatoes prospered near his house and they tasted most delicious;
my plot of back yard upturned by me, which had made my hands blis-
tered and unpleasant-looking, looked as if an animal of any kind had
mistakenly thought something was buried there and had sought in
vain to find it; no one looking at the mess I had made would think that
a treasure of any kind, long lost, had finally been unearthed there.

I moved into another house not too far away and with a larger
yard. Chet died and I am still ashamed that I never saw him again after
I left my old house, and also I never attended his funeral, even though
I knew of it, and when I now see his wife, Millie, she avoids me
(though I am sure I avoid her, too, but I would rather think that it is
she who is avoiding me). I moved to a house which had been the
house of someone named Mrs. McGovern and she had just died, too,
but I never knew her or even heard of her and so moving into her
house carried no real feeling of her for me, until one day, my first

spring spent in that new house and so in that new property, this happened: the autumn before, we had paid someone a large amount of money to regrade the lawn out back and it looked perfect enough, but that following spring lots of patches of maroon-colored leaf sprouts began to emerge from the newly reconstituted lawn out back. How annoyed I was, and just on the verge of calling up the lawn person to complain bitterly, when my new neighbor, Beth Winter, came over to see me and to talk to me about how enjoyable she found it to live with her family of a husband and three children in the very same house in which she grew up; on hearing of my complaints about the lawn person and seeing the maroon-colored leaf sprouts I had pointed out to her, she said, "But you know, Mrs. McGovern had a peony garden." And that was how I learned what the new shoots of peonies look like

and that was how I came to recognize a maple, but not that its Latin name is *Acer*; Latin names came later, with resistance.

That first spring in old Mrs. McGovern's house (but she was long dead) I discovered her large old patch of daylilies (*Hemerocallis fulva*) growing just outside the south-

west kitchen window and Rob (Woolmington) came with his modest rototiller and made a largish square with it for my vegetable garden and then followed me around the outside perimeter of the house with the same modest rototiller as I directed him to turn up the soil, making beds in strange shapes, so that the house would eventually seem to be protected by a moat made not of water but the result of an enthusiastic beginning familiarity with horticulture.

This is how my garden began; then again, it would not be at all false to say that just at that moment I was reading a book and that book (written by the historian William Prescott) happened to be about the conquest of Mexico, or New Spain, as it was then called, and I came upon the flower called marigold and the flower called dahlia and the flower called zinnia, and after that the garden was to me more than the garden as I used to think of it. After that the garden was also something else.

By the time I was firmly living in Mrs. McGovern's house (or the

Yellow House, which is what the children came to call it, for it was painted yellow), I had begun to dig up, or to have dug up for me, parts of the lawn in the back of the house and parts of the lawn in the front of the house, into the most peculiar ungardenlike shapes. These beds—for I was attempting to make such a thing as flower beds—were odd in shape, odd in relation to the way flower beds usually look in a garden; I could see that they were odd and I could see that they did not look like the flower beds in gardens I admired, the gardens of my friends, the gardens portrayed in my books on gardening, but I couldn't help that; I wanted a garden that looked like something I had in my mind's eye, but exactly what that might be I did not know and even now do not know. And this must be why: the garden for me is so bound up with words about the garden, with words themselves, that any set idea of the garden, any set picture, is a provocation to me.

It was not until I was living in Dr. Woodworth's house (the Brown Shingled House with Red Shutters) some years later that I came to understand the shape of the beds. In Dr. Woodworth's house, I had much more space, I had a lawn, and then beyond the lawn I had some acres. The lawn of Dr. Woodworth's house was bigger than the lawn at old Mrs. McGovern's house, and so my beds were bigger, their shapes more strange, more not the usual shape of beds in a proper garden, and they became so much more difficult to explain to other gardeners who had more experience with a garden than I and more of an established aesthetic of a garden than I. "What is this?" I have been asked. "What are you trying to do here?" I have been asked. Sometimes I would reply by saying, "I don't really know," or sometimes I would reply "............" (with absolute silence). When it dawned on me that the garden I was making (and am still making and will always be making) resembled a map of the Caribbean and the sea that surrounds it, I did not tell this to the gardeners who had asked me to explain the thing I was doing, or to explain what I was trying to do; I only marveled at the way the garden is for me an exercise in memory, a way of remembering my own immediate past, a way of getting to a past that is my own (the Caribbean Sea) and the past as it is indirectly related to me (the conquest of Mexico and its surroundings).

PART I

WISTERIA

*I*s there someone to whom I can write for an answer to this question: Why is my *Wisteria floribunda,* trained into a standard so that it eventually will look like a small tree, blooming in late July, almost August, instead of May, the way wisterias in general are supposed to do? The one that is blooming out of its natural season is blue in color; I have another one similar in every way (or so I believe), except that it should show white flowers; it does not bloom at all, it only throws out long, twining stems, mixing itself up with the canes of the *Rosa* 'Alchymist,' which is growing not too nearby, mixing itself up with a honeysuckle (*Lonicera*) and even going far away to twine itself around a red rose (*Rosa* 'Henry Kelsy'). What to do? I like to ask myself this question, "What to do?" especially when I myself do not have an answer to it. What to do? When it comes up, what to do (slugs are everywhere) and I know a ready-made solution, I feel confident and secure in the world (my world), and again when it comes up, what to do (the wisteria are blooming out of their season), I still feel confident and secure that someone somewhere has had this same perplexing condition (for most certainly I cannot be the first person to have had this experience), and he or she will explain to me the phenomenon that is in front of me: my wisteria grown as a standard (made to look like a tree) is blooming two months after its usual time. Do standards sometimes do that at first, when they are in their youth of being standards, the whole process of going from one form (vining) to another (a shrub, a small tree) being so difficult and unusual; in trying to go from one to the other, does the whole process of holding it all together become so difficult that precise bloom time becomes a casualty, something like appearing at the proper time to have your hair examined by the headmistress: you show up but your hair is not the way it should be, it is not styled in a way that pleases her, it is not styled in a way that she understands. What to do with the wisteria? should I let it go, blooming and blooming, each new bud looking authoritative but also not quite right at all, as if on a dare, a surprise even to itself, looking as if its out-of-seasonness was a modest, tentative query?

But what am I to do with this droopy, weepy sadness in the middle of summer, with its color and shape reminding me of mourning, as it does in spring remind me of mourning, but mourning the death of something that happened long ago (winter is dead in spring, and not only that, there is no hint that it will ever come again). Summer does have that color of purple, the monkshoods have that color, and they start blooming in late July, and I have so many different kinds I am able to have ones that will bloom all the way into October; but monkshoods do not look sad, they look poisonous, which they are, and they look evil or as if they might hold something evil, the way anything bearing the shape of a hood would. I like the monkshoods, but especially I like them because friends whom I love through the garden (Dan Hinkley, Annie Woodhull) grow them and grow them beautifully, and they are always saying how marvelous it is to have that particular kind of color in the garden (deep purple) at that particular time of the year (deep summer, late summer) and I see their point, but deep down I want to know, why can't there be a flower that is as beautiful in shape as the monkshood but in the colors that I like best: yellow, or something in that range. What should I do? What am I to do?

The supposed-to-be-white-blooming wisteria has never bloomed. I found two long shoots coming from its rootstock one day while I was weeding nearby and I cut them off with a ferociousness, as if they had actually done something wrong and so now deserved this. Will it ever bloom, I ask myself, and what shall I do if it does not? Will I be happy with its widish form, its abundant leafiness and the absence of flowers, and will I then plant nearby something to go with all that? What should I do? What will I do?

And what is midsummer anyway? What should I do with such a thing? I was once in Finland on the twenty-first of June, which was called midsummer, and I stayed up all night with some Finnish people and we went in and out of a sauna and we went in and out of a lake—the sauna was built on its shore—and then we went dancing at a place where there were some people who did not look like the Finnish people who were my hosts and the Finnish people called them

Gypsies. And the Finnish people kept saying that it was in this way they celebrated midsummer, in and out of a sauna, in and out of a lake, dancing in a dance hall along with other people called Gypsies. The buddleia 'African Queen' is said (by Dan Hinkley in his catalogue) to bloom in midsummer, but it bloomed before the late (and false) blooming wisteria and it bloomed just after the date of midsummer in Finland; the buddleia 'Potter's Purple' is blooming now in late July, but I had bought it because I thought it would bloom in late August to early September; and so what will I do then, when late August arrives (as surely it will, since I like it; but winter I do not like at all and so I am never convinced that it will actually return); to what can I look forward? The aster 'Little Carlow' (surely the most beautiful aster in the world) right now has formed flower heads, and they look as if they will bloom soon, any time now, but they bloom usually in late September to early October and they have a kind of purple/blue that makes you think not of sadness but of wonder: how can such a color be and what is that color exactly? What to do? The sedum, too, was about to bloom in late July, early August, and I am ignoring that the buddleia 'Pink Charm,' which blooms in early September and is planted especially for that, is about to bloom in late July, early August. What to do?

How agitated I am when I am in the garden, and how happy I am to be so agitated. How vexed I often am when I am in the garden, and how happy I am to be so vexed. What to do? Nothing works just the way I thought it would, nothing looks just the way I had imagined it, and when sometimes it does look like what I had imagined (and this, thank God, is rare) I am startled that my imagination is so ordinary. Why are those wonderful weeping wisterias (or so they looked in a catalogue: wonderful, inviting, even perfect) not fitting in the way I had imagined them, on opposite sides of a stone terrace made up of a patchwork of native Vermont stone? I had not yet understood and also had not yet been able to afford incorporating the element of water in my garden. I could not afford a pond, I could not understand exactly where a pond ought to go in the general arrangement of things. I do not even like a pond, really. When I was a child and living in another part of the world, the opposite of the part of the world in which I now live (and have made a garden), I knew ponds, small, really small bodies of water that had formed naturally (I knew of no human hand that had forced them to be that way), and they were not benign in their beauty: they held flowers, pond lilies, and the pond lilies bore a fruit that when roasted was very sweet, and to harvest the fruit of the lilies in the first place was very dangerous, for almost nobody who loved the taste of them (children) could swim, and so attempts to collect the fruit of pond lilies were dangerous; I believe I can remember people who died (children) trying to reach these pond lilies, but perhaps no such thing happened, perhaps I was only afraid that such a thing would happen; perhaps I only thought if I tried to reap the fruit of pond lilies I would die. I have eaten the fruit of pond lilies, they were delicious, but I can't remember what they tasted like, only that they were delicious and that they were delicious, and that no matter that I can't remember exactly what they tasted like, they were delicious again.

In my garden there ought to be a pond. All gardens, all gardens with serious intention (but what could that mean) ought to have water as a feature. My garden has no serious intention, my garden has only series of doubts upon series of doubts. What to do about the wisteria blooming out of turn (turn being the same as season)? And then just now I remember that I saw the *Lycoris squamigera* blooming also, and just nearby the (by now) strange wisteria, in late July, and it was at the foot of the wisteria; but it looked sickly, its bare stalk was stooped over, limp, its head of flowers opening almost, and then not at all. What to do? The lycoris had such a healthy flourish of green leaves resembling a headmaster's strap first thing on a school morning, before it had met the palm of a hand or a buttocks (not bare buttocks, they were shielded by khaki), in the spring, so abundant were they, that they made me worry about the ability of the *Anemone pulsatilla*, which I had so desperately pursued (I loved the blooms, I loved what came after, the seed heads, which perhaps can be appreciated only if you like the things that come after, just that, the mess that comes after the thing you have just enjoyed). And still what to do? Whom should I ask what to do? Is there a person to whom I could ask such a question and would that person have an answer that would make sense to me in a rational way (in the way even I have come to accept things as rational), and would that person be able to make the rational way imbued with awe and not so much with the practical; I know the practical, it will keep you breathing; awe, on the other hand, is what makes you (me) want to keep living.

But what to do? That year of the wisteria behaving not in its usual way, not in the way I had expected it to behave when I bought it based on its firm illustrious description in a catalogue, other events occurred. And so what to do? One afternoon, a proper afternoon, the sun was unobscured in its correct place in the sky, a fox emerged from my woodland (and it is my woodland, for I carved it out of the chaos of the wood and bramble and made it up so that it seemed like the chaos of the wood and bramble but carefully, willfully, eliminating the parts of a wood and bramble that do not please me, which is to say a part of wood and bramble that I do not yet understand). I had never seen a fox so close by at that time of day; I was startled (really, I was afraid of seeing something so outside my everyday in the middle of my everyday), I screamed; it is possible I said, "It's a fox!" The other peo-

ple who were in the house (the housekeeper Mary Jean and Vrinda) came out of the house and saw it also. When the fox saw us looking at him or her (we could not tell if it was a male looking for a spouse or a mother looking for nourishment), it just stood there in the shadow of the hedge (a not-accounted-for, yet welcome *Euonymus alatus*) looking at us, and perhaps it was afraid of our presence and perhaps it was curious about our presence, having observed us at times when we were not aware of it. The fox stood there, perhaps in the thrall of my shriek, perhaps never having heard such a thing as a shriek coming from the species to which I belong (I believe I am in the human species, I am mostly ambivalent about this, but when I saw the fox I hoped my shriek sounded like something familiar to the fox, something human). What to do when the fox looked at me as if he was interested in me in just the way I was interested in him (who is he, what is he doing standing there just a few steps from my front door, my front door being just a stone's throw from where he/she might be expected to make a den). The fox, after looking at me (for a while, I suppose, though what is a while really?), walked off in that stylish way of all beings who are confident that the ground on which they put their feet will remain in place, will remain just where they expect the ground to be. The fox skipped through the soft fruit garden, that section of the garden that I have (it was a whim) devoted to fruits whose pits can be consumed whole with a benefit that Adele Davis (she is now dead) might have approved.

What to do about the fox? The wisteria at the moment the fox appeared was not on my mind. The fox, seen in the shade of the euonymus, was gray in color, its coat looking like an ornament, a collar of the coat of someone who could afford such a thing, or a part of the handbag of someone who could afford such a thing, or a spectacle on the wall of someone who could afford such a thing and then not have the good sense to say no to it; when it (the fox) gallivanted into the part of the garden that was not in the shade, the part of the garden that was full of sun, he wasn't gray at all, his entire coat looked as if someone had just put a light to it, as if he had just been set on fire. The fox did not run away from me, only advanced away from me as I tentatively went forward. The way he would run away from me with his head turned toward me, watching me behind him as he propelled himself forward, was frightening: I cannot do that. And then he disappeared into another part of the wild and I could not follow.

What to do about the fox? For that spring, as I looked worriedly at the wisteria, seeing the little nubs along the drooping stems grow fattish and then burst open into little shoots of green, I saw a small round thing hopping behind some rosebushes (*Rosa* 'Stanwell Perpetual') and then disappear behind some pots in which I meant to grow sweet peas. The small round thing moved faster than a chipmunk, did not have a long tail, and so was more attractive than a rat; it emerged from behind the pots slowly, peeking, and then came out altogether and stared at me. It was a baby rabbit, and I could see (I felt I could see, I thought I could see) that he was not familiar with danger; he was not malicious and never (as far as I could see) ate anything that was of any value (ornamental or otherwise) to me; he was a pest only because sometimes, when I did not expect him, he would suddenly hop into my view, startling me out of some worry or other (I mostly worry in the garden, I am mostly vexed in the garden). His mother must have worried about him, because one day I saw her (I felt it was his mother, I thought it was his mother) looking for him. I saw them once emerging from the woodland part of the garden, I saw them again in the company of some other rabbits, and I could tell them apart from the other rabbits because none of the others were as big as the mother or as small as he. And then I didn't see them anymore and never even thought of them anymore, until that day I saw the fox emerge from the woodland. It still remains that I never see them anymore, but it does not remain so that I never think of them anymore. I thought of them just an hour ago, when I put three lobsters alive in a pot of boiling water, and it is possible that I will think of them tomorrow when I am eating the lobsters sometime during the day. Will the shells from the lobster be good for the compost? I will look it up in a book, I have a book that tells me what to do with everything in the garden, and sometimes I take its advice and sometimes I do not; sometimes I do what suits me, sometimes I do in the garden just whatever I please.

And what to do? For this summer was like no other and this summer was like all the others. I never had wisteria before; in any case, I had never had wisteria bloom in summer before, I had never heard of it. In this summer of the blooming wisteria the tomatoes (all heirlooms) yielded not abundantly, but they always do that—yielding not abundantly—and only when I taste them ('Prudens Purple,' 'Striped German,' 'Green Zebra,' 'Radiator Charlie') do I forget all complaints, only when I visit other people who, at the end of the season, have tomatoes lined up on newspaper all over their floors, tomatoes with no attribute other than "I grew them myself." This summer (and it is now that summer) I reaped a planting of peas ('British Knight') and then shortly after planted another batch (and that was a success also), and the cucumbers yielded more than I could use, but the potatoes, the early ones, the late ones, all got a blight and that is the way of potatoes in my vegetable garden, wherever I plant them, whatever their time of maturity, they get a blight, something or other that makes them not attractive if you see them just lying in a wicker basket, just picked, but they are delicious anyway when boiled and tossed in butter and parsley. The beets grew slowly, the carrots grew slowly, it rained too much and then it did not rain enough.

In the holding bed a young *Magnolia ashei* bloomed, one large white fragrant flower sitting in the middle of some larger leaves, but I noticed it only because . . . because, well, of how I wanted the wisteria to bloom; I had such a picture of it, the wisteria, blooming in spring with late bulbs, and the sound of that bird that is going even farther north, the sound that bird makes is sweet and piercing, as if pleasure could also be pain (as if pleasure is not also pain), the blue of the wisteria (blooming now, or then) on one side of the patio, its white counterpart on the other, with an underplanting of yellow tulips ('Mrs. J. T. Scheepers') and an almost full-blooming *Fothergilla gardenii,* and *Frittillaria persica* nearby. And when I saw the *Magnolia ashei* unexpectedly blooming, it made me long for the wisteria, and I wondered if I had done something wrong (horticulturally, though on the whole I never wonder, I know for certain I have done something wrong); but *M. ashei* blooms at a very young age; a book I have, entirely devoted to magnolias, *The World of Magnolias* by Dorothy J. Callaway, tells me so.

That summer, this summer! The wisteria came into bloom just at that moment in the summer, in the garden, when I could not imagine that there could be such a thing as winter, when the fact of winter seems amusing, like something malicious (short of death) happening to someone I dislike in an irrational way. Oh, winter, what is it, anyway? What is it really, this thing where the air is cold, the trees are bare, and all beings, human or otherwise, look hungry, look as if there is not enough of anything and there never will be. But just then, just now (that summer, this summer! when the wisteria was blooming out of turn), the leaves of the trees had reached a green beyond which they could not go, they were only going to be green, certainly so, and the lawn would no longer be lush with grass, only untidy and overgrown and need cutting, and, and . . . Oh, the deliciousness of complaining about nothing of any consequence and that such a thing should be the case in a garden: because, (again) that wisteria blooming now (or then) so close to the buddleia, which in turn is not too far from the *Phlox paniculata* 'Norh Leigh,' which is also somehow in the middle of the *Phlox paniculata* 'David,' is all pleasing to my eye, as I was looking at it then (now); at that moment of the wisteria, turning left or right (counterclockwise or clockwise), this is what I could see in front of me, this is what might be the zenith of summer in this (my) garden: the perennial pea (*Lathyrus latifolius*) in bloom in its guzzling way (eating up all the space around it and slightly beyond and then really beyond that); some cultivars of *Lobelia siphilitica* (bought from Dan Hinkley because I was so taken by his description, and I remain open to seeing this lobelia just the way Dan described it) on the verge of blooming; an accidental planting combination of *Platycodon grandiflorus* blue and pink; a large amount of a tall monkshood that I did not stake and so it has bent over and mingled with the perennial pea; and the perennial pea, which has sent up a set of only white blooms into the dry brown thing that had been the huge bloom of *Crambe cordifolia* (and how perfect, for I could never have done this: white replacing white on purpose); and the leaves on the vine of the *Clematis paniculata,* its pleasingly smelly blooms to come in early September (I think, in this the summer of the strange blooming wisteria); the very later blooming monkshood, the fading delphiniums (some of them from Dan Hinkley's 'Melissa's Hope' strain, some from Bob Stewart's recommended McClegnan's Hybrids), the *Malva* (*alcea* and *moschata*), which I did not like and now (then) feel as if I cannot live without and look at the clumps in other people's gardens with envy and obligatory admiration; the *Codonopsis clematidea* demanding that you bend over—bow—to see them if you want to do that—see them, they are worth that. And while still looking, my head going from right to left, I cross the pathway that divides this part of the garden (the pathway is a convenience), and on the other side of the pathway is pure hideousness, some cup plants, some plume poppies, and there are other things (a grouping of yellow hollyhocks, yellow trumpet lilies, yellow and close-to-yellow blooming kniphofia, but I like them); a much treasured tree tobacco plant (*Nicotiana glauca,* I believe, and not *Nicotiana tomentosa,* though I can't tell the difference and don't really care to); a banana tree (*Musa* 'Lord Cavendish') growing in a pot and looking happy amid a background of plants alien to it (evergreens, the monkshood); two pots holding the dark red, glossy-leaved dahlia 'Bishop of Llandaff' (gotten from Dan H.), the yellow-flowering bud-dleia; the ever-blooming rose 'Pristine'; the once-blooming roses 'Henry Kelsey' and 'Alchymist,' and the, for me, sometimes blooming 'Stanwell Perpetual'; two clematis of Himalayan origin from Dan H. (I cannot remember their names, only that he was so enthusiastic about their good qualities, and I can't remember those, only that I like them very much and do not know any other gardeners who cultivate them); the white wisteria, which did not bloom and so did not cause me any disturbance at all (it just threw out many vines, which I assume will grow into limbs, and then from there will come stems and on them . . . flowers?); and then the *Lilium orientalis* 'Black Beauty,' which is not black at all, but how I long for it to be that, black—a flower that is the color black, black like the night or like something that is instantly recognizably black is so rare that in the garden, in a flower, I long for it; and then, in this episode, in this part of the garden, I stop where the agapanthus 'Blue,' bred by the great Eric Smith, is in full bloom in a clay pot. How I love Eric Smith, especially since I know him only in the most impersonal of ways; I do not know if he preferred meat to vegetables or wool to cotton, I only know that most small-leaved blue hostas ('Halcyon' especially) are the product of his interests and efforts.

Oh, how I like the rush of things, the thickness of things, everything condensed as it is happening, long after it has happened, so that any attempt to understand it will become like an unraveling of a large piece of cloth that had been laid flat and framed and placed as a hanging on a wall and, even then, expected to stand for something. In this summer, in that summer, evenings would come on, and the birds would begin their annoying, or frightful (if I was in that mood), or cheerful (if I was in that mood), or simply birdlike noise, if I was in a mood to understand that a bird was often, itself, birdlike. There was a woodpecker, and one day while marveling or muddling (they were the same, really) over the wisteria, I heard its loud hammering and looked up and saw it picking away with its beak at the eave of my house. I love especially to sleep in the mornings until when the sun is almost in the middle of the sky, not quite, just almost, and sometimes, when I was asleep and in the middle of a most enjoyable dream, I would be awakened by that hammering, not the sound of the hammering of a carpenter who was repairing my wall, but a hammering all the same. A man who is not a carpenter makes a monthly visit to my house, and his visit has to do with controlling the presence of rodents inside the house (this is only a way of saying that he makes sure that rodents do not live inside my house and that if they try to live inside my house they will soon die). When this man, while looking at my house to see the places a rodent might find convenient to enter, saw the holes on the outside of my house left by the hammering of the woodpecker, he said to me, There are insects living in and eating up your house. What should I do? I said to him, and he said something, only now I have on purpose forgotten, for whenever I find a bird dead not far from my house, and in the garden, I wonder if it is because they ate the insects who were eating my house. I found the woodpecker dead in the yellow border; I found robins dead not far from the yellow border. What to do? I asked myself. And just when I was really perplexed, and engaged in an argument with myself about my own fears and my responsibility to others (birds, at that!), another woodpecker appeared and was hammering away at the house, and one day was so loud that I could not concentrate on my reading (I was reading Jeremiah, the Hebrew prophet). And then I found the broken shell of a robin egg in the dwarf evergreen beds, and something else, a bird whose name I did not know, built a nest just behind the red shutters of the window, and laid eggs there and the mother was very discreet, but her children were a perfect nuisance, especially at half past five in the morning.

And in that summer, this summer, in which the wisteria bloomed out of turn, it first rained too much, and then it did not rain enough, and then it rained too much again, and then it did not rain again, just not rain again, really. It was not a drought, and by a drought I mean absence of rain and at the same time a heat that purposely (maliciously) reaches deep into the soil and removes as much moisture as it can find, enough moisture to make me worry and then fret and then be vexed. The irritation to be found in the garden, the pleasure in it—

for it is not an irritation like the kind met when putting on a favorite dress after a little while and then finding that the buttons at the waist, or the ones that are supposed to secure the opening across the chest or the ones that are supposed to secure the opening at a vulnerable part in the back, are missing or simply won't go anywhere near the buttonhole—the irritation to be found in the garden will not lead to any loss of face; it will only lead to this question: What to do? and the happiness to be found in that!

The yellow border does not work; the aurelian lilies are too, are too . . . something, and the something is not quite right for the yellow border, they hang oddly; I have nothing in bloom at the same time to give them proper company. The kniphofia is in bloom at the same time as they (the trumpets are), but the kniphofia is not a good enough counterpart, the kniphofia should not be so near to the trumpet lilies. The yellow hollyhocks (*Alcea ficifolia*) are good towering above the aurelian lilies, but I do not have enough of them, for a reason (I could not afford to buy as many as I needed, or as many as I wanted) I always find humiliating: a lack of money. I do not like money, I only love the ability to dispose of it, and sometimes my disposing of it leads to some comfort for others, but mostly my disposing of money leads to much disappointment for me; for with me satisfaction is elusive (and so worth pursuing); for example, the horrible cup plant (*Rudbeckia maxima*) with its blooms the color of a universal yellow (and sometimes the universal is reassuring and uplifting and inspiring, and then again sometimes the universal is not, just not so at all). And in that summer, this summer! I had been traipsing around, tramping around in the gar-

den, looking at the failed yellow border (looking at how I had misunderstood the shapes and the colors of some things, the presence of
some things, the effect of all of them making a whole), I was in despair
(but again, of the pleasurable kind, the kind that everyone living in the
area of the world that starts in the Sudan and ends in southern Africa
ought to have, just to begin with). And in this traipsing up and down
with a gait that I must say has its own integrity (it certainly was outside and beyond the one I once thought proper when wearing a
Brownie uniform, when expecting to meet someone who at the
moment of their being born was better than I), I met another of my
misunderstandings: the *Carpinus betulus* 'Pendula' was doing very
nicely, thriving in its spot, which is in the middle of the middle of the
bed I have called 'Hispaniola'; but I have surrounded this beautiful
specimen, with its stout trunk like a strong backbone, I have surrounded this beautiful specimen, with its long, weeping branches and
corded leaves, with thalictrum and *Scabiosa ochroleuca* and
Filipendula 'Venusta' and plume poppy and some lobelia (ordinary
blue) and some turtlehead (pink) and some *Aster tataricus* and more
late-blooming monkshood and some *Eryngium yuccifolium* and the
poor thing, the *Carpinus betulus* 'Pendula,' that is, looked as if it had
found itself *orphaned* and in care of people who could not love it in the
way it had thought appropriate in which to be loved.

I moved the *Scabiosa ochroleuca* into the yellow bed—it is yellowish and tall and airy and wants to go everywhere it feels will be sus-
ceptible to its presence (I am reminded of myself, except for the
yellowish part). Next year, next season, in the summers to come (I
imagine myself in the summers to come, and I believe in my continued existence in the summers to come far less than I believe in the

fact that winter will come again), I imagine it airy, that is, moving in an undesperate way, in front of the climbing roses (*R. filipes* 'Kiftsgate,' 'Paul's Himalayan Musk,' and some other roses whose names I cannot recall and whose records of purchase I have misplaced), replacing the rudbeckia, making the kniphofia appear desirable ("How I should like to have those," a friend of mine will say), making the hollyhocks appear as if they were a new idea, giving the planting across the walkway (perennial pea, lobelia, delphinium, monkshood, platycodon, *Codonopsis clematidea,* the autumn-blooming clematis that had attached itself to the long-past large blooming heads of *Crambe cordifolia,* and then in early autumn will come small white star-shaped flowers smelling like honey or something like that, something that made you want to eat it or bathe in it). The *Scabiosa ochroleuca* would bring all this, my vision of that area of the garden to rest, the sort of rest that leads to satisfaction; the sort of satisfaction that leads to reflection and contentment (even if the contentment is disturbing, but it is the sort of contentment that leads to disturbance, the disturbance in the mind). The *Scabiosa ochroleuca* comes from east and south of Europe and in its *Scabiosa ochroleuca* self, I am sure it had not imagined my garden and the scheme I had in mind: it would brighten the hollyhocks (which were great by themselves without brightening but why not that—brightening, if only just to agree or disagree, brightening? not brightening?). I moved the *Scabiosa ochroleuca,* it immediately withered, starting from its top stem all the way to the ground. Next year (that summer, this summer!), when I see the results of my handiwork, the results of my vexations, I feel sure I will be irritated with the joy of success or deeply vexed by the results of my miscalculation.

THE HOUSE

*F*rom the house in which I live I can see a mountain called Mount Anthony from ten of my house's thirty windows. I do not know who this mountain is named after, but I don't think Anthony is such a distinguished name for a mountain. It's just that the name lends itself so easily to familiarity, and one shouldn't be on intimate terms with a mountain. Mt. Tony. I think this sitting inside my house looking at the mountain. I almost never really notice the mountain when I am outside my house. When I am outside my house, other things occupy me.

I love the house in which I live. Before I lived in it, before I was ever even inside it, before I knew anything about it, I loved it. I would drive by, seeing it sitting on its little mound, seeming far away (because I, we, did not own it then), mysterious in its brown shingles, its red shutters, surrounded by the most undistinguished of evergreens (but I did not know they were undistinguished then), humble-seeming, and that is how it drew attention to itself, by seeming humble. I longed to live in this house, I wanted to live in this house. I was a grown-up woman by that time, I had already had my first child and should have by then settled the question of where I should live and the kind of place I should live in, for that sort of settling down is an external metaphor for something that should be done inside, a restfulness, so that you can concentrate on this other business, living, bringing up a child. But I would see this house and long for it. It was especially visible in winter, for then the other trees that were not among the undistinguished evergreens were bare of leaves and the house would become more visible. These other trees, too, were without horticultural interest, common maples, the kind that seed themselves everywhere, choking each other out, distorting each other's trunk, chokecherry. In the winter the house is particularly beautiful when it is surrounded by snow, and the little mound on which it stands falls away from it, down into a meadow, and I would imagine my children (I had one child when I first saw the house but I knew I would have more, I always wanted to have more than one child, and the reason is completely selfish, but with children are there any other kinds of reasons) sliding down this slope in snowsuits, on sleds. This is now a sight I see quite regularly on a winter's day when there is snow on the ground and from the very same windows from which I view the mountain named after an Anthony.

A house has a physical definition; a home has a spiritual one. My house I can easily describe: it is made of wood (Douglas-fir beams, red cedar shingles), it has four bedrooms, a sleeping porch, two and one half bathrooms, a kitchen which flows into the large area where we eat our meals, a living room, a sunroom, a room over the garage where my husband works, another room in which I work. That is my house. My home cannot be described so easily; many, many things make up my home.

The house in which I now live was built in 1935 by a man named Robert Woodworth for himself and his wife, Helen, and their three children. I am very conscious of this fact, for almost every day something makes me so: the view of Mount Anthony, those uninteresting evergreens, when something, the plumbing, breaks and has to be repaired, the low cost of heating such a large house (it is well insulated), the room in which I write. He died in the room in which I write. A barometer, which he might have consulted every day, still hangs in the same place he must have put it many years ago. I have no real interest in the weather, only as it might affect my garden, and so I regard the barometer as a piece of decoration on the wall. Robert Woodworth was a botanist and taught this subject at a nearby college. He invented time-lapse photography. I do not know if the exciting and unusual collection of trilliums, jack-in-the-pulpit, squirrel corn, Solomon's seal, and mayapple that are in a bed just outside the kitchen window are the very same ones that appear in his films on time-lapse photography. He tended a vegetable garden and also raised chickens. There was a henhouse right near the vegetable garden, but I tore it down after much agonizing, for it was a beautiful Vermont-like structure, which is to say, simple, calling attention to itself by its very simplicity, just like the house. I loved the henhouse. I believe I was not around to see it actually being dismantled.

There are people alive who remember the house being built by

Robert Woodworth himself, without an architect's advice; his three children, three boys then, very grown-up men now, for instance; a man who sells real estate remembers how, as a small boy, he went with Robert Woodworth to borrow a backhoe from the town to make the hole in the ground that would become the foundation. It is an excellent foundation, people who know about such things constantly tell me so. The middle son tells of the difficulty of making the hole in the ground; the backhoe then was not the powerful smooth machine that my son, Harold, is so in love with now; it took much manual manipulation. Also, the Vermont soil is mostly rocks. The youngest son remembers that later, after the house was completed and they were living in it, his father thought that Helen, Mrs. Woodworth, the mother of those three boys, would enjoy a sunroom, and he watched as his oldest brother helped his father build an addition to the house, a room with exposed beams and a stone floor, for the purpose of a woman sitting as she took shelter from the hot summer sun. This room, the sunroom, has a spectacular view of Mount Anthony; it also has some special windows that slide open with a curving motion instead of just moving straight across. I was told by someone, an architect, that most carpenters would find this kind of window difficult to make today. These windows are impossible to open and shut with that modern birthright: convenience; but I can never replace them, certainly not the way I have replaced the storm windows in all the other windows in the house. Those windows had storm windows that had to be removed in the summer and replaced in the winter. My husband and I had many quarrels over whose chore that should be. He grew up in a city in an apartment building and was used to calling a servant to perform tasks that no one in his family could or would perform; I grew up in a climate in which windows were open and shut for the purpose of keeping out light or letting in light, and such a chore could be performed by anyone capable of it, that is, even a child.

It is through the emotions of the youngest of these three men who grew up in the house in which I now live, his lasting attachment to the house in which he grew up, that I view my house. He remembers when those ordinary, unimpressive evergreens were planted; he remembers how big they were in relation to his own height at the time they were planted. He will look at the trees, the evergreens, and he will place his hand somewhat above his head and say that he remembers them being that much taller than he was when they were planted. He was, of course, smaller than he is now, for he was a boy then and he is a man now, but when he sees the trees and when he speaks of the trees, he is speaking of things that he is perhaps conscious of, perhaps not, but that are not being communicated clearly, and should not be communicated clearly. He is speaking of a mystery. Where did the trees come from and why did his father plant them? They have no real interest to me, they are not unusual in any way. I once had a botanist come and look at them, a botanist who is a successor to Robert Woodworth at the college where he used to teach. The botanist said the trees were not of any real interest; just ordinary hemlocks, Norway spruce, pines. This botanist meant that there was nothing of botanical interest planted near my house, but he had never seen the youngest son of Robert Woodworth measure his grown self against the grown tree. To see the top of the grown tree now, the grown man has to arch his head way back until it is uncomfortable to swallow while doing so, and then he cannot hold such a pose for too long. I once invited a man to dinner, a man who knows a lot about landscape and how to remake it in a fashionable way. He did not like the way I had made a garden and he said to me that what I ought to do is remove the trees. It is quite likely that I shall never have him back for a visit to my house, but I haven't yet told him so. After he left I went around and apologized to the trees. I do not find such a gesture, apologizing to the trees, laughable.

Some of the people who were children in the house in which I now live were very sorry to have it sold out of their family. I understood their feeling so well that I told them they could come back and see the house any time they wished, and I also told them that if we were ever to sell our house we would call them all, the children of the Woodworths, the grandchildren of the Woodworths, and offer to sell it to them first. We, my husband and I, believe that we shall never live anyplace else, certainly if we can help it, but we can't really tell what we will be able to help or not help, we only know that we believe we shall never live anyplace else. When the Woodworths were clearing out the house, after it had been sold to us, different people took things that meant something to them. One grandchild took a bed that she had slept in when she came to visit her grandparents; someone took fireplace implements because they were unusual and because of some special memory. I do not know who took the reproduction of an engraved print depicting the Puritan legend of Miles Standish and Priscilla Alden. When we were dismantling Mrs. Woodworth's kitchen, someone asked us to look for recipe cards that might have fallen behind her old kitchen counter; they remembered something with meringue and kept asking us if we were sure when we said we had found nothing. Someone took cuttings of Mrs. Woodworth's roses because they had come from her mother's garden in Maine many,

many years ago. I cannot believe that my children will return to this
house shortly after I am dead (I do believe that I will live here for the
rest of a very long life) and ask the new owners (for my children are
Americans and Americans are unable to live adult lives in the places
they are born) to try to retrieve the copy of Edna Lewis's cookbook
from which our family have enjoyed the recipe for corn pudding and
fried chicken and biscuits; nor will they ask for the four volumes of
Elizabeth David's cookbooks, in which are recipes for food our family
have enjoyed, not the least being something called Summer Pudding,
a dessert made of currants and stale bread, the berries foreign to me
until in my adulthood I have grown them, and the bread distasteful to
me, though only through the memory of my own childhood; or the per-
petually leafed-through but never actually used *Mrs. Beeton's Guide to
Household Management*. I cannot imagine my children will actually
want to admit that they came from us and did not fall out of the plain
blue sky, which is just what I used to wish when I became aware that
to have me, my parents actually had sex. Just the other day my husband overheard my daughter say to her friends as he approached her
and some other girls all huddled together, "Oh, here comes my dorky
dad." He was humiliated to hear himself referred to as a dork, and so
he said to the other girls, "Hi. Now, do I look like a dork?" and instead
of saying in unison, "No, you are the most wonderful father we have
ever had the good fortune to meet," all the girls simply looked at the
tips of their shoes in what he interpreted to be silent agreement. But
our children are still children, one is six and the other is ten. They perhaps think we will live forever, they perhaps think we will never go
away, that they will never be able to be themselves without our
reminding them of their own helplessness, their own dependence on

us. Perhaps pies with a meringue topping and summer puddings are missed only when they can never be had in a particular and exact way again.

The ways small events work are interesting only to the small-minded. All small events are domestic events, and domestic events are those events that can occur in any area in which it seems quite all right to expel saliva. If I were asked to make a definition of domestic space, I would say that domestic space is any space in which anyone might feel comfortable expelling any bodily fluid. Of course, to have bodily fluids which must be expelled one must have an intake of some substance or another. It is here that Edna Lewis and Elizabeth David and Mrs. Beeton are a great help. The world turns on the small event. Everybody who does anything leaves home. This action, leaving your home, has an effect on the person, on the people left behind, and, sometimes most dramatically, on the new people one meets. And then again, if the world turns on small events, the small event only modifies you, only you are affected by it.

It was one very early morning in January, four years ago, when I was running with my friend Meg and we came to a point in our conversation where we had to stop running because of the emotions expressed about, specifically, our children (she has three, I have two) and, in general, the world (between the two of us there is only one of those, the world), when suddenly I saw the house I now live in looming out of the newborn daylight. I was standing perhaps a hundred yards away from it, but at that moment it seemed far away, shrouded by a forest of those insignificant evergreens (it seemed a forest then, but in reality there are very few) and of course shrouded by unfamiliarity, because I had never been inside it, I had only longed to live in it, I had seen this house only from the street and longed to live in it. When I saw the house that morning while running with my friend Meg, I said to her, "I wish I lived in that house," and she replied, "You know, that's Robert Woodworth's house and I think I just read in the paper that he died. I bet that house is for sale. I bet his children don't want it." It is only now I can think of the luxury of a man dying and his children choosing to dispose of the substantial things he might have left for them, choosing only to keep the recipes for pies, cuttings of old roses, choosing memories, as opposed to the real thing, the house. Robert Woodworth's children did want to sell the house. They were sad about it, they had loved their father and they had loved their mother, they had loved living in this house, their own children had loved spending summers with their grandparents in this house. But Robert Woodworth's children are Americans; Americans will not live in the houses where they were children.

Buying Robert Woodworth's house plunged us, my husband and me, into a crisis. We were living in a house that we had outgrown: we had started out living in it as a family of three: a mother, a father, a two-year-old girl. By the time I had expressed my longing for Robert Woodworth's house to my friend Meg, we had become a family of four. That house was at least twenty times as big as the house I grew up in, a house in a poor country with a tropical climate, but I had lived in America for a long time and had adjusted to the American habit of taking up at least twenty times as much of the available resources as each person needs. This is a trait that is beyond greed. A greedy person is often cross, unpleasant. Americans, at least the ones I am personally familiar with, are not at all cross. They are quite happy and reasonable, as they take up at least twenty times as much of everything as they need. For four people we needed a bigger house. We decided then that we should sell our house to enable us to buy Robert Woodworth's house. We consulted a real estate agent and she told us that we should ask for an amount of money that was many times more than we had paid for our house. It was expected that we would make a profit. But no one would buy our house, not at the price we asked, not at a little less, not at a lot less. Our house sat there. Each day we prayed someone would come and buy it, each day we prayed that no one else noticed the Woodworth house sitting there empty, how beautiful it

was, how happily they could see themselves living there. My family and I had one small advantage, one small blessing: the Woodworth children seemed to favor our having the house, because my husband is a composer, and from their childhood memories of their mother, Helen, playing the piano and their father, Bob, playing the banjo, they imagined the house with us in it would be filled with music, the way it had been when they were children. They were right. The house is often filled with music, though from time to time it is the music of a group called Green Day, Annie and Harold's favorite band. As each deadline for that part of the house buying/selling ceremony called "passing papers" came and went, we would call the Woodworth children, anxiously explaining our plight, and they would reassure us that they would wait a little bit longer before putting the house into another house-buying ceremony called "the market."

One day, seven months after I was running with Meg and saw Robert Woodworth's house and expressed the longing to live in it, two young people came to look at our house (it was painted yellow, a yellow common to yellow houses in Finland, not the yellow of the Caribbean, the place I am from; this was a deliberate choice on my part and I was expressing something quite common; which is, liking the thing you are not). They offered an amount of money that we accepted immediately and this made them suspicious, for they had thought that there would be that other house buying/selling ceremony, the counteroffer. I was so eager to leave my old house that I left behind some *Paeonia* 'Festiva Maxima' that had been given to me; they were divided from a plant that was fifty years old. It is only now when I drive by my old house in June and see them blooming away that I am filled with regret that I did not say to the people buying my house,

"Yes, that price will do very well as long as I can take my 'Festiva Maxima,' for they are not only the most beautiful of peonies, they are the first flowers I isolated and became attached to at the moment I became a gardener."

I cannot now remember the day on which the house we used to live in was sold; and I cannot remember the day on which Robert Woodworth's house became our house. I can only remember that not one of the heirs' domiciles could accommodate Helen's piano. It was offered to us for purchase, but we could hardly afford the down payment on the house and so had to decline. It now sits in our living room waiting for permanent settlement with one of Helen's grandchildren. My children practice their piano-lesson assignments on it all the time. Many quarrels are had over Helen's piano. They do not like to practice their piano lessons, apparently no child who lives in the culture of piano playing and who has imposed on him and her the love of music through the piano ever likes practicing the piano. And so this piano is yet another reminder of the people we call the Woodworths.

If you must go through your life being reminded of people you have never met, Bob and Helen Woodworth would be the ideal people with whom to have this experience. At Robert Woodworth's memorial service there were many people from the small village of North Bennington. Some of them were colleagues of his from the college where he taught, others were just local people whom he had known from being a resident of the village. I'm not sure they noticed how many of their memories of Robert Woodworth were like this: "Bob and I were chopping wood" or "I gave Bob some wood" or "That day Bob called me about some wood." I was sitting in the audience and I believe I was the only person who had never met Bob Woodworth, and so that must have been why I noticed that there were a lot of memories about wood connected to a man named Woodworth. I desperately wanted to stand up and point out the connection between the wood and the name of the person being commemorated. I did not. All the people who talked about him mentioned how close he was to Helen and how much they all loved Helen, too. He played Dixieland music with a group of men every Tuesday night. One night, the last Tuesday night before he died, he said goodbye to them and one man said to him, "See you next week, Bob," and Robert Woodworth said, "I don't think so." And that was true. He died sometime between that Tuesday night and the next Tuesday night when they would meet. The man he had the exchange with told that story at his memorial service. After we bought the house, we went through it and found a lot of wood ready for the fireplace in the basement. In the basement also was a wood-burning stove and it was hooked up to the furnace. We realized that the entire house could be heated with wood, but no one in my family is capable of cutting it.

When Dr. Woodworth died in the room in which I now write, he was alone. Helen had died two years earlier. His spirit does not haunt the room. His spirit does not haunt the house. One night, during the first winter we spent in the house, I was lying in my bed, when suddenly I smelled smoke. I ran into every room, I ran into the attic, I ran into the basement, trying to see where the smell of smoke was coming from, trying to see if I could find the thing burning. The smell of smoke was not to be found in any other part of the house, only in my bedroom. The phenomenon of the smell of smoke occurs only in the wintertime and only in that one room.

When I lived in the yellow house, I used to pass other houses and imagine myself in them. I used to see the other houses and love some of them; sometimes I wished I lived in them. Some of them were very beautiful all by themselves, or they were beautiful and in an extraordinary setting to boot. I never do that anymore. I never want to live anywhere else or in any other house.

But I do not believe that I know how to live in a house. I grew up outside. All my meals were cooked outside on the top of a stove-like implement made from clay called a coal pot. Then we must have grown a little more prosperous, for we acquired a kerosene stove; it had a wick that it was my duty to keep trimmed. There isn't a room in my house now that is as small as the house I grew up in. I can hardly believe that this is so, but it is really, really true. We lived outside. When we started to do things together inside our house, things other than sleeping, it was a sign of some pretension. I remember when I started to eat my meals inside with my family. I was taught to set the table. When I did anything bad, I was banished from the table and had to eat my meals outside under a soursop tree. I still do not like this fruit. Most of the things inside the house in which I grew up were thought to be very valuable. I was not allowed to touch them. Our good things were in trunks or in a mahogany cabinet that my father had made. My mother had a set of six china teacups and matching saucers commemorating the coronation of some monarch of England or another and they were locked up in that cabinet. My father made wonderful furniture, but we didn't have his best furniture. His best furniture was in the house of the wife of the man with whom he had apprenticed as a cabinetmaker, and he and my mother had almost as many quarrels about him retrieving that furniture as she and I had when she found me almost removing her coronation tea set. It was as if the house in which his furniture was kept from my mother were the cabinet that kept her china from me.

When I go to other people's houses, I am amazed at the order there. Their sinks are clean, the countertops are neat, the curtains match something or other and they are a nice length. Their children have never battled imaginary adversaries on the sofa with their shoes on. Their books are all in place on their bookshelves. My house looks quite like the outside in which I grew up. The outside in which I grew up had an order to it, but this order had to be restored at the beginning of each day. This restoring was done by my mother and by me as I grew up, for my mother was training me to do things the way she had done them (there was nothing sinister in that, everyone who is good at anything likes an apprentice). In the middle of my yard stood the stone heap, and this was covered with soapy white clothes on Monday mornings. This stone heap was a mound of stones about a foot high, and I do not now know its diameter but it was properly wide; the stones, which were only stacked one on top of the other with no substance to hold them together, would come apart, it seemed during the night, and from time to time they had to be rearranged. In my yard was a latrine, and on Wednesday nights the night-soil men would come and take away its contents; they came on horse-drawn carts, and the clop-clop of the horses and their loud talk always woke everyone up. They were very disrespectful of the sleepy comfort of the people inside, but such consideration would have been possible only if they had been saints; they were not, they were merely night-soil men. They never locked the gates behind them, they trampled on things even when they were not directly in their way, the yard had to be tidied up after them. In the yard, too, was the soursop tree, and it was under these branches that

I was banished to after I had committed some infraction, the most memorable for me being the time I dropped my brother in what seemed an accident to me but not to my mother, shortly after he was a year old. There was also a clump of sugarcane that was desirable to my mother at first but later fell out of her favor, and since she could not simply get rid of it, she would pour boiling water constantly over its crown; and a pawpaw tree and a dumps tree and a coconut tree; and there was a coal pot and in it a fire made from charcoal that my mother had bought from a woman named Mrs. Roberts, who lived in a village called Old Road, and this woman and her husband, a Mr. Roberts, made the charcoal from the wood of trees that they had cut down, and I do not believe that they, Mr. and Mrs. Roberts, worried about the management of woods and their effect on the general arrangement of things in the small world in which we lived, never mind the small world of the yard. On the soursop tree grew a squash vine (crookneck squash), the seeds of which I now see are offered for sale in distinctive vegetable catalogues; this was an important vegetable in our daily diet, and naturally, I could not stand it. I liked it as much as I liked breadfruit, but at the time I could not have known that my dislike of breadfruit was perfectly reasonable. A breadfruit tree grew in our yard, and my mother, who was obsessively familiar with such things as the nutritional value in kinds of food, knew of the breadfruit's nutritional value; I did not know of the breadfruit's history, but all the same my palate had a revulsion to it that was shared by every Antiguan child I have ever met.

My mother would preside over the yard with an agitation that perhaps is endemic to people in her situation. The dishes are clean, then they are dirty, and then they are clean and then they are dirty. The stone heap will not stay in its immaculate mound. The night-soil men will never close the gate, it must always be closed after them, for if it is not, evil spirits will find it much easier to enter our yard and wreak havoc with our lives. The leaves never stay on the trees, they are always yellowing and eventually falling down and then have to be swept up in a pile and then taken away. Nothing behaves, nothing can be counted on to do so. Everything eventually becomes smudged, falls out of place, waiting to be restored. All of this was my yard. And all of this continues outside my house today, only the details have changed. The collection of stones has been made into a wall; the trees are different, but they provide more or less the same function of usefulness and pleasure. Only, this area outside my house today is called the garden.

The inside of my house looks like my yard; it is smudged with dirt, it is disorderly for an inside of a house, though it would look wonderful and memorable if it were the outside of the house I grew up in, even though perhaps it would not be appreciated by anyone I grew up with, their standards being on a level I can never meet, and even more deeply, fervently hope never to meet. The standards of my past are marvelous for the people I left behind and anyone else wishing to join them. They are good standards, they are admirable standards, only they do not fit me anymore.

"Harold," I can hear my husband say, "no playing with that stick." Harold is our son and he is playing outside, roasting marshmallows on a fire built in a coal pot, the very same kind of coal pot on which all my meals used to be cooked, only now on a visit to the place in which I grew up I sought one out and bought it the way a tourist would. "Harold," I can hear my husband say again, "don't play so near the fire with that stick." I hear shrieks of pleasure from Harold, which can only mean that he is getting near the fire, nearer than his father finds comfortable, but the closer to danger is the closer to pleasure for a child, and perhaps for everybody who has ever been a child, and perhaps again, almost no one quite forgets this. I can remember that my mother was once ironing my clothes and that the irons, all four of them, were kept hot by the fire in the coal pot. I was dancing around the coal pot in an imaginary Maypole dance and my mother kept saying, "Don't dance around the coal pot, you might fall into the fire," when suddenly I did fall into the fire, and to this day the scars from that burn are visible around my elbows. What did I learn about fire that I did not already know? Fire burns flesh; if you are a child you will feel it. Harold never did fall into that particular fire.

What does one teach a child, what should a child know? In our home we are not sure. Robert Woodworth must have known; his children are all safe and sound and no one has anything but good to say about them. We live in Robert Woodworth's house, the home he gave to his children; they can do their best and pass something of it on to their children, but when they sold us the house, they could not sell us the home also. A home is not tangible, a home is not the Douglas-fir beams, the cedar shingles, the windows from an admiral's house in Massachusetts.

Is this a home? One day, when Harold was just a baby, really a baby, and so Annie would have been just over four years old, Annie overheard her father and me discussing the various opinions of a man, and in this discussion we decided that the man was a homophobe. I can remember that her father said, "I'm afraid he's a homophobe, there's no doubt about it." And I said I agreed. At that moment Annie

was sitting on the kitchen table, something she was not allowed to do for a reason that even now that she is almost eleven years old is not at all clear to me; only that it seems a child should not sit on the kitchen table. We knew of her presence, but we did not think of her as we spoke, we did not think that the things we were saying would mean anything to her. There is a moment when you are the parent of a child and you forget this, you still think you are alone in the world and you behave as if you are, and you act as if you are. When Annie said, "Wait a minute, wait a minute, what is a homophobe?" we were shocked to hear her voice, we thought we were talking to each other alone.

It was her father, Allen, who said—and these were his exact words, I so far have never forgotten them—"Well, you see, Annie, it's like this. Two men meet and they fall in love with each other and they decide to get married. That's homosexual. Then over here, you have some people who don't like the two men who have fallen in love and decided to get married. They are afraid of it. When you are afraid of something, that's a phobia. So the people who are afraid of two men who decide to get married, they are homophobic." And Annie said in reply to all this, "Wait a minute, two men get married, right." Her father said, "Yes." And she said, "Just tell me one thing, who wears the veil?" Her father said, "They decide." And Annie said, "Oh."

In our home, which is in a house that Robert Woodworth built, a man none of us have ever met, a man no one will ever really know, for it turns out that no one can ever be really known, we wish that someone had told us what to do, but no one has left a blueprint. We wish someone had. We wish we could say, Well, Bob Woodworth did it this way and it was very satisfactory, because one of his children is a podiatrist, and another is a professor of biology, and another is a scientist and lives a life of stability somewhere south of Burlington, Vermont, and that seems so manageable from our point of view as parents, because those three people are people we are able to have a conversation with, even though all three of them are people we would have been afraid of becoming, if only because the stability of such lives reminds us of our own youth. Oh, how we wish that someone, but perhaps Robert Woodworth in particular, had given us a recipe for how to make a house a home, a home being the place in which the mystical way of maneuvering through the world in an ethical way, a way universally understood to be honorable and universally understood to be ecstatic and universally understood to be the way we would all want it to be, carefully balanced between our own needs and the needs of other people, people we do not know and may never like and can never like, but people all the same who must be considered with the utmost seriousness, the same seriousness with which we consider our own lives.

THE SEASON PAST

I was putting the garden to bed for the winter when, looking over the empty spaces that had not so long ago been full of flowers and vegetables, I was overcome with the memory of satisfaction and despair, two feelings not unfamiliar to any gardener. Satisfaction was seeing the tips of the asparagus poke through the earth, coming all the way up, wonderfully whole, real, and without blemish, just the way they should be really, from the trenches into which I had placed their roots. Even after many years of gardening, I never believe a live plant will emerge from the seed I have put in the ground; I am always surprised, as if it had never happened to me before, as if every time were the first time. And a moment of despair was when I realized that none of my squash and pumpkin seeds were germinating, so no plants would appear, because some beings, full of malice, had carefully scratched the seeds out of their hills and eaten them. I plotted the demise of the offending beings, and finally did catch one of them, a raccoon, in that ridiculous pantywaist contraption, the Havahart trap. But when I was about to drown him in a barrel of water, the three whining pacifists I have somehow managed to find myself living with (my husband and our two children) made such a fuss that I ended up setting him free in wilderness far away from anyone's garden. (I do believe, though, that some natural instinct, not fully understood by any scientist, will lead him back to mine.)

My 'Reine des Violettes' and 'Madame Isaac Pereire' roses, planted just last April, were glorious in the summer; the perfume of the 'Violettes' in particular was extremely pleasing, really faultless; I kept burying my nose in its petals as if they were someone's neck. And the 'Madame Isaac' was remontant, it bloomed on and on. The dimensions of my foray into rose growing were unknown to me until the beginning of April, when they started arriving; by early May, there was a total of thirty-three bushes. I had not ordered them all at once; the excess came about because last winter was so long and cold and I had so much time to stare at catalogues that I lost track of what I had already ordered and ended up with sometimes two or three schemes for the same spot. I had ordered my roses from Jackson & Perkins, Wayside Gardens, and Park Seed (Park has the cheapest roses, and they seem just as good as the others, but the selection is more limited; my wonderful 'Reine de V.' came from them, it was five dollars less than in the Wayside catalogue), and from a nursery in Maine called the Roseraie at Bayfields, run by a very pleasant man named Lloyd Brace. (I know that he's nice only from talking to him on the telephone.) When the rosebushes arrived, I had not yet prepared the ground properly for them, because it was still freezing and snowing. So they were badly mistreated before planting, and looked half dead by the time they were planted, except for the ones from Lloyd Brace, which came with fresh sprouts of green leaves on them and looked exceptionally promising when they were finally in the ground. All the roses did well, anyway, making me think—contrary to my expectations—that abuse must be a part of growing roses.

This business with the too many roses began two summers ago, when I received a letter from Jackson & Perkins inviting me to become one of the people in the United States to choose the best of the new roses they were introducing that year. In a brochure that came with the invitation, some people testified to the pleasure they had had while participating in this venture, and they were so effusive that at first I thought they must have got the roses free; they had not. For a reason not at all clear to me, I am drawn to the activities of people I do not want to know or meet and would never befriend, and so, of course, the minute I saw this brochure I sent my money away so that I, too, could become a member of the Rose Test Panel. The competitors arrived at the same time as all the other species, but they didn't have proper names; they were labeled 'Pink Blend,' 'Pink,' 'White,' and 'Yellow.' I planted them, and at first I observed them closely, for I expected to receive a bothersome diary and, when that didn't happen, a phone call and, when that didn't happen, some form of communication from Jackson & Perkins soliciting my observations about these roses. I forgot about the Test Panel; other problems became overwhelming: the canes of the 'Souvenir de la Malmaison' (which I got from Wayside) grew tall and then fell over onto the lawn, and it would not bloom; I had read Peter Beale, who said of it: "This rose at its best is the most beautiful of all Bourbons, but at its worst it can be horrid. It hates wet weather and in such conditions seldom opens properly without help." I had been staring for a long time at the multitude of flopped-over canes when it dawned on me that what I was looking at was not a 'Souvenir de la Malmaison' at all but something else altogether, something that had perhaps been misnamed. Not so very long after that, I received another letter from Jackson & Perkins inviting me to join *next* year's Rose Test Panel. Actually, through a lack of communication between Jackson & Perkins and me, I had never voted on the four roses I had grown, and this left me with little enthusiasm for judging the Jackson & Perkins roses of the future.

The rose with which I had the most success was the 'Yellow,' though it isn't one I would tell people they must have. A rose I *would* recommend is 'Ballerina'; all summer I watched it send out sprays of dappled-pink blossoms on long apple-green canes. I had planted it next to some clethra, and for a while they were in bloom together, so I actually got a small glimpse of a something I had planned.

Just as I was mulching and covering up the roses for winter, I came upon Christopher Lloyd saying in the increasingly beautiful-to-look-at *Gardens Illustrated:* "I got fed up with all the trouble roses bring in their train. They get a lot of diseases and you can't replace a weak bush without changing the soil. They're quite disagreeable and make a very spotty effect even when they're flowering—a whole series of blobs. The climbing ones are quite shapely but the bush roses are pretty ugly." It's so appealing, the capriciousness of a gardener! I see that I shall be overwhelmed by the number of roses I will have ordered by next spring, so that twenty years hence I will firmly denounce the whole idea of growing roses.

I returned from a visit to the old suitcase (England) in May and found my hedge of common rhubarb in an incredible state of bloom, the tall stems covered with panicles of white; I stared at it in awe, as if I had never seen anything so beautiful, but I had. It then faded, of course, but not quite away; it turned brown—a deep, crisp, alive

shade, a tropical not a temperate brown—almost as if in defiance, for everything else was in a state of fresh, young green. I cut it down to the ground, and it grew back, so that by the tail end of summer, I was able to eat some rhubarb again, but this seemed all wrong, all out of context: when the days are getting longer is the right time to eat rhubarb.

In early June, perhaps giddy from observing the rhubarb and planting various things, I went to the store to buy milk, and on my way out bought three packets of nasturtium seeds. I had wanted to plant something along a walkway that leads to the door on the south side of our house—something that would spill over the slabs of marble in a happy, haphazard way—and the moment I saw the seed packets I knew the nasturtiums would do. They turned out to be one of the great pleasures of my growing season. I planted them very close together and I did not thin them but instead pruned and trained them to grow only in one direction: out onto the walk. They must have loved where they were, for they thrived. At night, the smell from them— sweet, like something fermenting that when consumed would make you crazy—was delicious. I considered my walkway a great triumph and was on the verge of bragging about it, but then, looking through Wayne Winterrowd's most helpful book of annuals (*Annuals for Connoisseurs*), I saw a photograph of nasturtiums spilling out onto a walkway in Monet's garden. At first I felt wonderful that I had had the same idea as a great gardener, and then, unable to help myself, I felt envy, because his nasturtiums had turned out much better than mine. His looked like a painting—the way all natural beauty looks. Mine were just a planting of nasturtiums.

A prostrate-growing evening primrose (*Oenothera missouriensis*) that I found at the Equinox Valley Nursery in Manchester, Vermont, was spectacular. I had never grown this particular primrose before and so had never seen the cycle of its amazing bloom: it has thick red stems from which sprout fat green pods (buds), sometimes with large red spots on them, and each pod breaks open at dusk to reveal a huge bubble of perfectly simple yellow, which by the middle of the next day has become a limp, slimy thing, like a squished caterpillar. (I made my son, Harold, hold one, and when he did he said, "Oh yuck!") Also at Equinox, I found a pink evening primrose (*Oenothera* 'Rosea'). It is about ten inches high, with small narrow leaves that turn beautifully red in fall; it spreads rapidly and is already all over the bed, but this will be just fine, because it is at the foot of the hollyhocks and musk mallow and sidalceas. That corner of the garden—hollyhocks, musk mallow, and sidalceas, with the roses 'Cécile Brünner' (both climbing and shrub) at one end and *R.* 'Ballerina' at the other—was meant to be a mass of varying shades of pink, but the sidalceas turned out to be a horrid shade of lilac, not at all the pink that I had seen in the catalogue. I deserved this: I got them from a puffed-up plants-man's outfit in Connecticut, where the people are very rude and high-handed on the phone. Of course, they would not take the sidalceas back. They were also quite skeptical when I said that a Canada lily they had sent was another kind of lily altogether. They replaced it in the fall with what they said were bulbs, but I have never seen bulbs like that, and if these odd-looking things fail to turn into plants, I can't imagine calling the company back to tell them so. This is a big contrast to my rapport with the people at Wayside, who are always eager to help, and make amends for every fault that's found; they even send letters of apology. (It's possible that this is an example of the way climate influences modes of behavior; does warm air inspire servitude? Wayside is in North Carolina.)

Another disappointment: one day a shipment of three-and-a-half-foot twigs arrived, apparently the hundreds of dollars' worth of fruit trees that I had ordered from a fruit-tree grower in upstate New York. They seemed such a far cry from the overladen-with-fruit trees I had seen in the catalogue that I almost burst into tears. I planted them on what was, for May, a severely cold and windy day; and a huge emptiness opened up before me: I thought, Between this planting and the reaping (I hope) to come, I will fill the time up, but with what? I did not know the answer, and this inspired such a state of anxiety that I had to lie down.

It was on another day altogether that I ended up in a similar state of anxiety for a very different reason. I was taking an indirect route going to the grocery store and I came upon a field of joe-pye weed in bloom. I had recently started bringing mullein into my garden, and when I felt I had enough of those, I started raiding my own field for joe pyes and bonesets. I love these flowers, and when I saw the field of joe pyes, it made me feel so happy and giddy, because it was so unexpected (I had no idea any were growing there). Then, when I got to the store, I heard the woman who waited on customers say to the man ahead of me, "Hi, honey. God, you're beautiful today," and this struck me as untrue, because I had seen the man quite clearly. After he left I said to her, "What made you say that to that man? He was one of the ugliest men I have ever seen," and she replied, "That was my husband." Retracing my route on the way home, I was so blind with humiliation and anxiety and shame that I did not even see the joe pyes.

I was eating a plate of common Blue Lake green beans in August, and they were extremely delicious; I had never grown them before, and I realized that I almost never grow ordinary vegetables. I have become so confident of having a constant supply of food that often when I decide to grow things I can eat they have to transcend the ordinary: they must have a different color from the usual; they must have a different shape; they must come from far away; they must be the favorite food of the people in the countryside of France or Italy, or in the mountains of Peru. It was this perversity that led me to grow French Marmande tomatoes, as well as some other tomatoes, which looked like large gooseberries (called 'Green Zebra,' and they were the best tomatoes I have ever tasted), and various odd potatoes—one called 'Russian Banana,' other kinds that looked like fingers, or were blue-skinned, or were pink when mashed. I also grew some cucumbers that were juicy and sweet and are ordinarily grown in Turkey or Syria (or somewhere near those places), and some purple beans that turned a disappointing green when cooked.

In early September I picked and cut open a small, soft, yellow-fleshed watermelon, and I was suddenly reminded of the pictures of small girls I used to see in a magazine for girls when I was a small girl myself: they were always at a birthday party, and the colors of their hair and of the clothes they wore and of the light in the room were all some variation of this shade, the golden shade of the watermelon that

I had grown. I would wish then to be a girl like that, with hair like that, in a room like that— and the despair I felt then that such a thing would never be true is replaced now with the satisfaction that such a thing would never be true. Those were the most delicious melons I have ever grown.

The leaves turned yellow and red and brown, and then fell; the days grew short; the heat from the sun grew thin, then just wasn't there anymore at all. I planted six different kinds of fritillaria, and some flag iris, and some peonies—ordinary ones, not trees, that looked spectacular in the catalogue I ordered them from. Then one day the long chill arrived, the chill that no heat can penetrate. Winter.

READING

It was a day in late October and I had two thousand dollars' worth of heirloom bulbs to place in the ground (the daffodils 'Empress of Ireland,' 'Beersheeba,' 'Beryl,' *Telmonius plenus*, 'Queen of the North'; the tulips 'Mrs. John T. Scheepers,' 'Queen of Night,' *Tulipa clusiana, T. turkestanica; Iris bucharica*), when almost one foot of snow fell on the ground. I do not like winter or anything that represents it (snow, the bare branches of trees, the earth seeming to hold its breath), and so I disliked the ground being covered with this soft substance (sticky and at the same time not so), with a color so definite (white) as if it wished to dispel any doubt that might arise in regard to this particular quality (its color, white). But snow will occupy all the spaces you know, the space above the ground, the space below the ground, and if you try to turn inward, as long as it is in front of you, it will occupy that space, too. For me, to look at a landscape covered with this substance is to look at despair, and I cannot find anything in the history of human beings to make me feel that my view is merely personal (I grew up on an island in a climate that is tropical and therefore am prejudiced). All I see when I look at the history of human beings is that people who find themselves living with this substance, snow, and the stilled landscape that comes with it, go South or long for the warmth that comes from living in the Southern Hemisphere. I feel that I can state this with some certainty only after helping my son make a map of the travels of Eric the Red and Lucky Leif Eriksson. This is the evidence I have for my feelings, but my own history contradicts this: I come from south (far south, I come from the West Indies) of where I now live, and I love the event called spring and accept that it comes after winter and that it cannot come without winter.

The snow so early did not go away; the snow stayed and the air grew colder and so winter started in mid-autumn. I began to complain and make a big fuss about this, but when I took a look at a pathetic journal of climate that I keep and make entries in from time to time, I saw that each year I say the same thing; winter always starts at about the same time (mid-autumn) and I always feel that this is unusual, that it comes too soon. The ground became harder and harder and harder still; the *Cyclamen hederifolium* (planted in the shade of an old hemlock) looked diminished, old; how could I have imagined that such a thing as cyclamens could ever really grow properly in my climate; except that I know they will come back along with the *Arum italicum,* which looks sort of similar, the leaves dappled with white and generous in shape in the way of leaves that belong in the tropics.

The surprise, the shock, of winter has become to me like a kiss from someone I love: I expect it, I want it, and yet, Ah! For it holds the expectation of pleasure to come: spring, yes, but most immediately the arrival of catalogues with their descriptions and illustrations of the familiar (achillea, campanula) desperately attempting to and actually succeeding in sounding like something new, something you must order right away even as it lies outside in your garden, dormant. You can imagine its roots tight and stilled beneath the ground, if you just look out your window; it is building up the resources to emerge with a vigor (in the seemingly fabled spring) so frightening you secretly consult your memory on the one-through-four steps of dividing plant material.

I walked around my garden with such thoughts on my mind. Some of them I think are recurring, some of them new, but the new eventually recur if I garden long enough, for the garden repeats itself all the time and will advance only so long as human history and all that it entails moves along also. The earth was folded shut and I was at first shocked, but then remembered it from before; the sun was weak, not stinking with heat, not threatening a fire of extinction, erasure, but I remembered that, too, from before. By now I have been gardening for years, and memory, ephemeral, subject to things I hope not to understand, is for me an anchor. Walking around the garden, then, I am full of thoughts of doom, I am full of thoughts of life beyond my own imagining. I come inside.

On this particular day the mail was mostly from my creditors (garden related), first gently pleading that I pay them and then in the next paragraph proffering a threat of some kind. But since there was no clear Dickensian reference (debtors' prison), I wasn't at all disturbed, and when I saw that along with the bills there were some catalogues, all caution and sense of financial responsibility went away. The best catalogues of any kind, whether they are offering fruits, vegetables, flowers, shrubs, trees, will not have any pictures; the best nurserymen in this country will not sully their catalogues with lavish pictures but will only now and then print some little illustration of a leaf, a bird perched on a limb of something, a pail (empty or full, it won't matter), a watering can; the best nurserymen will sometimes not give you any information on growing zones or instructions regarding cultivation; the best nurserymen just assume that if you are interested in what they have to offer (all of it so unusual, it is sometimes not to be found yet

in any plant encyclopedia) they will be chatty enough about it; they will be full of anecdotes in regard to the season just past, but they will not show you a picture and you certainly will not have a little passport-size photograph of them grinning up at you.

And so it was with a certain confidence and happiness that I grabbed my catalogue from Ronniger's, a seed and potato company in Moyie Springs, Idaho. This used to be my favorite catalogue in the world; it made people with whom I am sure I would never agree on anything of importance seem wonderful. But the current catalogue makes me hesitate. For one thing, it is almost twice as long as it used to be (forty pages then, seventy-two pages now), and the new pages are taken up with things I would never buy from Ronniger's anyhow: ornamental alliums, asparagus, and blueberries. It even now has a color advertisement for some soon-to-be-useless garden implement (I know this, I have the very same one in my garage, it is broken). The worst part is a picture of Mr. Ronniger crouching down next to some potatoes he has just reaped: I can see his teeth, so he must be smiling, and the picture has a caption that says "Harvest is a time of great joy." If I am disappointed in Mr. Ronniger's new catalogue, will I now be disappointed in the potatoes, too? For not all the potato seeds will be grown by him; the ones grown by him will be labeled "Organically Grown," the ones grown by someone else will be labeled "Certified Seed."

A nice ballast to shore myself up from the emotional devastation (well, from a gardening point of view) endured during the careful reading of the potato catalogue was reading the entire six volumes of the Mapp and Lucia saga written by E. F. Benson. There is nothing I like more than reading about malice and gossip and life in a small village (I only like to read about it, though, I should not like to live in it myself). And so fortified, I returned to my favorite catalogues, the ones without pictures and captions and instructions for cultivation. In the Heronswood catalogue the plantsman Daniel J. Hinkley writes nicely about a recent seed-collecting trip he made to Japan; he writes that he saw five different species of *Acer* in the wild and apparently they were new to him, and also that a single specimen of *Schisandra nigra* loaded with fruit caused him to stop as if dead when he saw it. This catalogue and the Arrowhead Alpines catalogue is all an American gardener with intense interest would ever need. The nurseryman at Arrowhead Alpines is Bob Stewart, and he has a wife named Brigitta and a son named Ender; he has a friend who is a professor at a nearby university and that friend had an unusual clump of *Petasites,* certainly it was unlike any I had seen before, and he got the professor to sell some to me. One year Bob began his letter to his customers by telling us he had finally gotten rid of his first wife and the financial demands she made on him by offering her a large settlement; she accepted, but he did not say how much it was; I really did want to know.

The grimness of winter for this gardener can be eased only by such things. On my night table now is a large stack of books and all of them concern the Atlantic slave trade and how the world in which I live sprang from it. The days will have to grow longer, warmer, and softer before I can pick one of them up.

THE GARDEN IN WINTER

One summer, early in the afternoon, I went to visit my friend Love. She and her mother (a perfectly nice woman, just to look at her) were walking in her garden. (Love's garden is in the shape of an enormous circle, subdivided into long and short rectangular-shaped beds, half-circle-shaped beds, square-shaped beds, and it is separated from her house by a wide sheet of obsessively well-cut grass and a deep border of iris, foxglove, and other June/July flower-bearing perennials.) Love was in a fretful mood (her mother's presence had made her that way) and was looking forward to seeing me (she told me so) and feeding me dinner, because I like the food she cooks (and in summer it is almost always something she has grown herself) and also perhaps because my presence would be a relief (this was not said, she did not tell me this). As Love and her mother walked around, they removed faded flowers, plants, and vegetables that were ready to be harvested (because Love grows vegetables and flowers quite freely together) and exchanged the silences and sentences typical of people who are bound together in a way they did not choose and cannot help (and so do not like), when her mother came on the bed where the Asiatic lilies were in bloom and broke one of their exchanges of silence by saying to her, "Just look at these nigger colors." Love was shocked by her mother saying this, but not surprised; after all, this was her mother, whom she had known for a long time.

Not so very long after Love and her mother had been walking in her garden, I arrived, and while Love stayed in the house and made us cocktails and small snacks of vegetables and a dip, her mother and I walked through the garden, because I had asked to do so (I always walk through Love's garden, but usually it is by myself), and her mother and I exchanged monuments of praise to Love's gardening ability, and when we came to the bed of Asiatic lilies, I was visibly listening to Love's mother tell me some not very important piece of gardening information (I cannot remember it now, and so that is why I say it was not very important), but to myself I was wondering if, since I did not know her very well and was not very sure if I liked her, I should be my natural and true self or unnatural and untrue with her. Without being conscious of which self I had decided upon, I blurted out something true. I said, pointing to the Asiatic lilies, "I hate these colors." And then I went back to being unnatural and untrue, and would have forgotten that entire afternoon altogether except that after dinner, while Love and I were doing the dishes alone, she vented to me some of the irritation she felt toward the many people in her life whom she loved but did not like. She told me of her mother's casual

but hateful remark, and I became so annoyed with myself for not sens-
ing immediately the true character of the person with whom I had
taken a walk in the garden, for had I known, I would have embraced
the Asiatic lilies and their repulsive colors with a force that perhaps
only death could weaken. If someone will go to such lengths to nour-
ish and cultivate prejudice, extending to an innocent flower the malice heaped on innocent people, then I certainly wouldn't want to be
the one to stand between her and her pleasure.

And then! The stone wall (visible from the back door of my
house) that sensibly separates a terrace and a large flower bed from a
sudden downward shift of the ground (but this is very nice to have, for
when it snows my children like to slide down it) was in a dilapidated
state and needed rebuilding. Two men, one overly fat, the other overly
thin (this Jack Sprat style in couples is not an unusual sight in
Vermont), came to rebuild it. One day, as they worked, I sat on a stone
step (also in need of repair) observing them, reveling in my delicious
position of living comfortably in a place that I am not from, enjoying
my position of visitor, enjoying my position of not-the-native, enjoying
especially the privilege of being able to make sound judgments about
the Other—that is, the two men who were stooped over before me,
working; and then I roused myself out of this, because I had to tell the
overly fat man to save for me some of Mrs. Woodworth's roses (which
he had dug up in the process of completely dismantling the wall; they
weren't especially pretty roses, but they had been in that spot for over
forty years and before that they had come from Mrs. Woodworth's
mother's house in Maine and I had a feeling about them, a sentimen-
tal feeling that was completely false, a feeling no native can ever afford
to have), and after I had told him that and he agreed to save the roses

for me, he told me that he had been to New York City only once in his life and didn't wish to go there again. And I made an instinctive decision to not make a reply, so he said that when he was a boy in school he had been to New York City on a day trip with his class, and on their way back home the bus he and his classmates were riding in had been pelted with stones by some people; and he said that not all the people who threw the stones were colored; and I said, Oh, but I wondered what he really wanted to say, and then he said that he liked colored people but his father did not. I said, Oh, to that, too, but I wondered what it was he really wanted to say; he said that his father did not like colored people because he was in the army with some colored men and they all got along very well until they were ordered into battle, and all the colored men in unison turned and ran away, and ever since then his father had not liked colored people. And then I was sorry that I had shared my organic cashews with him earlier that day, and I was sorry that I had brought him a nice glass of cold spring water to drink after he ate the cashew nuts; I said to him that it was so sensible of the soldiers to run away, I would most certainly have done the same thing, and he said nothing to that; and then I said that it was just as well that the soldiers were colored, because if they had been people who looked like his father (white), then most certainly his mother would have been someone who looked like me. And he stared at me and stared at me and said he saw what I meant, but that couldn't be true at all, because I couldn't see right away what I meant. The next day he brought me a small paper bag full of bulbs, each the size of three thimbles, and he did not know the name of the flower the bulbs would bear, he described it (small, white, star-shaped), and he said it would bloom early in the spring, much before anything else. I had wanted to plant the bulbs he gave me quite near the stone wall, and so I waited for the wall to be finished. And then the wall was finished and the paper that held the bulbs fell apart because I had left it unprotected on the ground and the bulbs spilled out and were scattered all over; at the beginning of each day as I began to work in the garden I would promise myself to plant them, at the end of each day I would resolve to myself to plant them; and then one day, with gestures that were completely without anger, I took the bulbs and placed them in the rubbish bin, not the compost heap.

It is winter and so my garden does not exist; in its place are these mounds of white, the raised beds covered with snow, like a graveyard, but not a graveyard in New England, with its orderliness and neatness and sense of that's-that, but more like a graveyard in a place where I am from, a warm place, where the grave is topped off with a huge mound of loose earth, because death is just another way of being, and the dead will not stay put, and sometimes their actions are more significant, more profound than when they were alive, and so no square structure made out of concrete can contain them. The snow covers the ground in the garden with the determination of death, an unyielding grip, and the whiteness of it is an eraser, so that I am almost in a state of disbelief: a clump of lovage with its tall, thick stalks of celery-like leaves (with celery-like taste) did really stand next to the hedge of rhubarb; the potatoes were near the rhubarb, the broccoli was near the potatoes, the carrots and beets were together and near the potatoes, the basil and the cilantro were together and near the peas, the tomatoes were in a bed by themselves (a long, narrow strip that I made all by myself this summer with a new little tiller I bought, separating my garden from Annie's (my daughter); the strawberries were in a bed by themselves; all the salad greens were together and in a bed by themselves; the sunflowers, tall and short, and in various hues of yellow and half-brown, were clustered in groups over here, over there, and over here again; the scarecrow that scared nothing was here, the gun to shoot the things the scarecrow didn't scare was right here (lying in between the bundles of hay that were used to mulch the potatoes), unloaded, as was the line of silver (aluminum pie plates strung together) between the tepees covered with lima-bean vine (they bore pods but they were empty of beans). These colors (the green of the leaves, the red/pink stem of the rhubarb, the red veins of the beet leaves, the yellows and browns of the sunflowers) start out tentatively, in a maybe, maybe-not way, a sort-of way, and then one day, perhaps after a heavy amount of rain, everything is strong and itself, twinkling, jewel-like, and at that moment I think life will never change, it will always be summer, the families of rabbit or woodchuck or something will eat the beet leaves just before they are ready to be picked. I plot

ways to kill them but can never bring myself to do it, I decide to build a fence around the garden and then I decide not to, there are more or fewer Japanese beetles than last year, who can really care; there are too many zucchinis, who can really care; and then, as if it had never happened before, something totally unexpected: I hear that the temperature will drop to such a low degree it will cause a frost, and I always take this personally, I think a frost is something someone is doing to me. This is to me how winter in the garden begins, with a frost, yet another tentativeness, a curtsy to the actual cold to come, a gentle form of it. The effect of the cold air on the things growing in the garden is something I still cannot get used to, still cannot understand, after so many years; how can it be that after a frost the garden looks as if it had been to a party in . . . hell; as if the entire garden had been picked up and placed just outside the furnace of a baker's oven and the fire inside the oven was constantly being fed and so the oven door was never shut.

I must have been about ten years old when I first came in contact with cold air; where I lived the air was only hot and then hotter, and if sometimes, usually only in December, the temperature at night got to around 75 degrees, everyone wore a sweater and a flannel blanket was placed on the bed. But once, the parents of a girl I knew got a refrigerator, and when they were not at home, she asked me to come in and put my hand in the freezer part. I became convinced then (and remain so even now) that cold air is unnatural and man-made and associated with prosperity (for refrigerators were common in the prosperous North) and more real and special than the warm air that was so ordinary to me; and then I became suspicious of it, because it seemed to me that it was also associated with the dark, with the cold comes the dark, in the dark things grow pale and die; no explanation from science or nature of how the sun can shine very brightly in the deep of winter has ever been satisfactory to me; in my heart I know the two cannot be, the cold and the bright light, at the same time.

And so between the end of summer and the shortest day of the year I battle a constant feeling of disbelief; everything comes to a halt rapidly, they die, die, die, the garden is all brown stalks and the ground tightening; the things that continue to grow and bloom do so in isolation; all the different species of chrysanthemums in the world grouped together (and some of them often are on display in a greenhouse at Smith College), all the sedum, all the rest of it, is very beautiful and I like it very much, but it doesn't really do, because it's against a background of dead or almost dead.

People will go on and on about the beauty of the garden in winter; they will point out scarlet berries in clusters hanging on stark brown brittle branches, they will insist that this beauty is deep and unique; people try to tell me about things like the Christmas rose (and sometimes they actually say *Helleborus niger,* but why? the common name sounds much better, the way common names always do), and this plant in bloom in December is really very beautiful, but only in the way of a single clean plate found on a table many months after a large number of people had eaten dinner there; or again they tell me of the barks of trees, in varying stages of peeling, and the moss of lichen growing on the barks of other trees and the precious jewel-like sparkle of lichen at certain times of day, in certain kinds of light; and, you know, I like lichen and I like moss, but really, to be reduced to admiring it because nothing else is there but brown bramble and some red stems and mist . . . It is so willful, this admiration of the garden in winter, this assertion that the garden is a beautiful place then. Here is Miss Gertrude Jekyll (with whose writing I am so in love and am always so surprised when I see a picture of her again to realize how really quite ugly she was; and then again, she is such a wonderful example of the English people's habit of infantilizing and making

everything cozy: a nice grouping of nut-bearing trees cannot remain a nice grouping of nut-bearing trees, they become The Nutwalk): "A hard frost is upon us. The thermometer registered eighteen degrees last night, and though there was only frost the night before it, the ground is hard frozen . . . How endlessly beautiful is the woodland in winter! Today there is a thin mist; just enough to make a background of tender blue mystery three hundred yards away, and to show any defect in the grouping of near trees."

But this is not true at all (of course, not to me); I want to say to her (but I can't, she's dead): This is just something you are saying, this is just something you are making up. I want to say that at this very moment I am looking out my window and the garden does not exist, it is lying underneath an expanse of snow, and there is a deep, thick mist, slowly seeping out of the woods, and as I see this I do not feel enraptured by it. But you know, white is not a color at all (the snow is white, the mist suggests white), white only makes you feel the absence of color, and white only makes you long for color and only makes you understand that the space is blank and is waiting to be filled up—with color.

It is best just to accept what you have and not take from other people the things they have that you do not have; and so I accept that I now live in a climate that has four seasons, one of which I do not fully appreciate, certainly from a gardener's point of view; what I would really like is to have winter, and then just the area that is my garden would be the West Indies, but only until spring comes, the season I like best, better than summer even. That is what I would really like. Since I cannot have it, I hope never to hear myself agreeing with this: "I determined to bring life to my garden in winter—to make autumn join hands with spring. Winter was to be a season in its own right, vital to the gardener who really wants to garden. I decided, like that innovative gardener, William Robinson, to banish the idea that 'winter is a doleful time for gardens.' " This is Rosemary Verey, and it

is from her book *The Garden in Winter*; there was not one idea or photograph in this book to make me change my mind, and besides, this is
just the sort of thing to give pleasure a bad name. The effort to be put
into finding beauty in a dry branch, a leafless tree, a clump of limp
grass, the still unyielding earth, is beyond me and not something I can
do naturally, without inner help.

One very cold night this winter, I had just had dinner with my
friend Kristen in a dreary restaurant in Bennington (but it's dreary only
because they won't change the menu; year in and year out, they serve
the same dishes, and though they are very good-tasting dishes, they are
always the same; I write hostile letters to the chef, but they remain in
my head, I never send them), and just as we were walking toward our
cars, she pointed to a charred stalk, the remains of a purple coneflower
(I had seen it in bloom when it had been in bloom), and she said, "Oh,
that's so great. You know, I have decided to plant only things that will
look good when they are dead and it's cold in my garden." Again this
sense of the effort involved came over me and I thought of the lilies in
my friend Love's garden. The reason I do not like those lilies is that
years ago, when I was young, for a period of about a year I used to take
a hallucinogenic drug at seven-day intervals; near the end of the year
I was doing this, the hallucinogenic part of the drug had no effect on
me, I experienced only the amphetamine part of it, and my stomach
would be in a state of tautness and jitters at once. This hallucinogenic
drug was sometimes square, sometimes round and glassy, and would
fit well in the middle of my tongue; it was sometimes yellow, sometimes orange, the exact shade and texture of Love's lilies. I never fail
to see those flowers, their waxy texture, their psychedelic shades,
without becoming aware of my stomach. Over dinner I had been dis-

cussing with Kristen how overwhelming I found the beginning of winter, the middle of winter, the end of winter, and how much I missed
my garden, and she mentioned seasonal mood shifts (those were her
words exactly) and the number of mood modifiers that were available
to the average person today. She said the word "Prozac" and I remembered that in response to something someone had said, I heard Fred
Seidel (he is my son's godfather) say that Prozac was the aspirin of the
nineties, and then not long after I heard Fred say that, I saw this drug;
it was in the palm of a druggist's hand, he was showing it to me; I had
asked him to show it to me; it was two-toned: a slight shade of green
and a smudged white, winter colors, colors from "nature's most sophis-
ticated palette" (Rosemary Verey). When my friend and I parted, she
was still in a state of admiration over the asleep and dead before her,
the remains of a fire by ice. At that moment I was thinking, I want to
be in a place where people don't say things like that, I want to be in a
place where people don't feel like that, see a landscape of things dead
or asleep and desire it, move mountains to achieve its effect; by tomorrow I want to be in a place that is the opposite of the one I am in now.
The only thing was, I did not know if that place would be a mood mod-
ifier or the West Indies.

EARTHLY DELIGHTS

What does a gardener need? I cannot say; I know only what I have needed in the garden. I am an absentminded person; that is, less charitably, I am a careless person, who mistreats her gardening equipment, leaving it to the elements—the rain, dew, and sun. I accidentally bury various digging or weeding utensils in mounds of dirt, and leave pruning shears, gloves, even plants somewhere that I mean to be a temporary resting place but that often turns out to be the place of their permanent abandonment. I use my books about the garden in almost the same way I use the other things connected to it. My copy of Peter Beale's *Roses* is tattered and smudged, because I read it while I am in the middle of planting or weeding or watering. I read it then because reading is the thing I like most to do and because I cannot imagine having an occupation that does not go along with reading, which is just as well, since I need an occupation to support my habit of reading. Above all, I believe that anything you need, or love, you must have more than one or two of. Love itself must be had in such a large amount that it eventually causes you to be sick of it.

Let me say again, I started to plant things—this is not the same thing as being a gardener—when, to celebrate my second Mother's Day, my husband, on my daughter's behalf, gave me some packets of seeds (I only remember delphiniums and marigolds), along with a rake, a hoe, and a digging fork, all bought from the Ames department store in Bennington, Vermont. I went outside, dug up the yard, and put the seeds in the ground. The skin on my right forefinger split, the muscles in the back of my calves and thighs were sore, and the digging fork broke; for all that, the seeds did not germinate, the yard of that house being mostly in the shade of old maple trees. Since then I *have* become a gardener, and here are some of the things I have come to love and need.

Among the first things I acquired was a good set of hand tools—
a trowel, a dibble, a cultivator, and a weeder. I believe I got those from
Smith & Hawken. I do not now have that same dibble or that same
cultivator; the ones I have now are from Langenbach, a gardener's-tool
outfit in Stillwater, New Jersey.

A canvas bag designed for carrying such things is a good idea,
especially if you can remember to put them in it to begin with; but any
old bag will do quite well, just as long as it can take dirt and water and
look the better for it. Ideally, my gardening bag contains lots of twine
for tying things up and for marking out rows; a small pair of scissors
for cutting the twine; a penknife; gloves and gloves, since in my experience no two of them ever make a pair (I can add that the ones from
Womanswork, of York, Maine, are the best I have ever had); a box of
wall nails specially designed for tacking up roses or other stout vines
against a wall or a post; a small hammer, almost toylike in size; a wire
cutter; a stapler, which is useful when I am making temporary fences
in the vegetable garden for vines of one sort or another to run up;
wooden labels; and an indelible-ink marker.

A visit to a botanical garden or a museum is another kind of gift
for a gardener. A most unexpected example might be a visit to the
Botanical Museum at Harvard, to view the fruits and flowers made of
blown glass which are on display there. The specimens of fruit are
shown at various stages of development, from blossom to their full
ripeness, and then in various stages of decay and disease; the specimens of flowers, however, are shown without any blemish at all. These
fruits and flowers, decaying or unblemished, are all beautiful, and, as
is the way of likenesses, seem more representative of the real than do
the things that they are meant to resemble. The creation of these sim-

ulacra is also an almost defiant assertion of will: it is man vying with nature herself. To see these things is to be reminded of how barefaced the notions of captivity and control used to be, because the very fabrication of these objects, in their perfection (no decay or blemish in nature is ever so appealing) and in the nature of the material from which they are made, attests to a will that must have felt itself impervious to submission. How permanent everything must feel when the world is going your way! It was in this museum that I discovered a book by the botanist Oakes Ames, who in his day knew a great deal about orchids. It is called *Jottings of a Harvard Botanist.* Ignore the introduction and the foreword, one by his daughter, the other by his grandson—yes, staple the pages together, as I do to the introductions of all books I am going to read. Oakes Ames is a personality you want to meet as if by accident, on some mode of public transportation (and leave him there). He was a nineteenth-century man of European descent: his sense of possession is funny now only because he is dead. On his way to Cuba, to visit Harvard's botany station there, he wrote this to his wife, Blanche: "We are surrounded by the usual uninteresting people one meets on a journey to Cuba and back; people who are well enough to watch, but undesirable to meet." This is the kind of confidence you have when the world is yours.

And this brings me to books, which are the things I most like to get. They are also, regrettably, the things that I am given only one of, because it must seem ridiculous to give somebody more than one copy of the same book. Yet I would very much like to have two copies of *The Graham Stuart Thomas Rose Book*—one for when I am sitting inside my house, dry and comfortable, and one for when I am tramping around my garden in the rain and mud, or walking through the sprin-

kler while it's on. I read my books, but I also *use* them; that is, sometimes the reading is almost a physical act. All of Graham Stuart
Thomas's books are books every gardener should have, not only
because he is so knowledgeable but also because he is deliciously
authoritative and overbearing in his opinions, the way people who
really know their business can't help being. And surely all of us, especially gardeners, must have someone whose advice and opinions we go
against, even at our plants' peril. Thomas's *Rose Book* (his *The Old
Shrub Roses, Shrub Roses of Today,* and *Climbing Roses Old and New*
have been combined into this one volume and reprinted by
Sagapress/Timber) is perhaps the essential book for a gardener interested in roses. It is not encyclopedic, like the Peter Beale's, but is
limited to the roses Thomas knows well. Personal experience and
botanical history blend in his sentences: "Well remembered, too, is the
day on which I purchased my first rose—'Mme Caroline Testout,' followed by other Hybrid Teas, now outclassed; they were recommended
by an uncle who was something of a connoisseur, and in whose garden
every rose bore, to my great satisfaction, a cast metal label." I've found
that when I'm reading this book a copy of the Pickering Nurseries
catalogue (of Pickering, Ontario) is good company. Sometimes his
description is so tempting (he says this about 'Guinée': "deepest
murrey with crimson centre, pure, unfading, without purple; beautiful
shapely flowers and intense red-rose fragrance") that I want to have
the rose being described; often I can find it in the Pickering catalogue.

My fascination with the authoritative and the overwhelmingly
confident compels me also to share my love of *Wyman's Gardening
Encyclopedia,* by Donald Wyman, *America's Garden Book,* by James
Bush-Brown and Louise Bush-Brown, and all books by Gertrude

Jekyll. With Wyman, the bullying begins in the first sentence: "A pleasing, well-grown garden reflects the personality of its owners, living proof that they have an interest and enthusiasm for growing plants, that they have an inherent feeling for design and good color combinations, and that they have a knowledge of horticulture." With the Bush-Browns, the bullying begins in the title: *America's Garden Book*. Can there then be any other? Obviously not. With Jekyll, the bullying sounds like this: "Every year that shows the experience gained by recent observation in the arrangement of plants for colour, confirms the conviction of the great value of a judicious use of what, for want of a better name, I know as the 'between' plants—plants that are not for bloom, but for some quiet quality that shall combine with and enhance the colouring of those that are near." I cannot resist anyone who can write such a sentence.

I have been to Sissinghurst; I have read Jane Brown's *Sissinghurst: Portrait of a Garden;* all the great gardeners I know love this garden and everything connected to it, especially its creators, Vita Sackville-West and her husband. It is a beautiful garden, an extraordinary creation. And yet I remain unmoved by it. Perhaps that is because I have read too much of Sackville-West's own writing. The best of her garden writing has been collected by Robin Lane Fox, an extraordinary gardener himself, in an anthology called *The Illustrated Garden Book*. I suspect that the source of my antipathy to Sackville-West and her garden is to be found in her observations of the garden, in the way she manages to be oblivious of the world. For the fact is that the world cannot be left out of the garden. At least, I find it to be so: that is why I regard Nina

Simone's autobiography as an essential companion volume to any work of Vita Sackville-West's. There is no mention of the garden in Nina Simone's account of her life, as there is no mention of the sad weight of the world in Sackville-West's account of her gardening. One is a life so dramatic that it seems very difficult to dramatize; the other has so little drama in it that, long after it is over, there is nothing left but silly dramatizations. And yet, and yet, in the way that it is worthwhile for any aspiring jazz singer to listen to Nina Simone, it is worthwhile for any gardener to look at the garden through Vita Sackville-West's eyes.

The painter with the best-known garden is, of course, Claude Monet. Everyone I have ever met who has a garden has something growing in it from seeds that were gathered in Monet's garden. Usually, it is hollyhocks. This makes sense: the seeds of hollyhocks are very easy to steal. (When I was going through a public garden in Ukraine this September, I saw some hollyhocks whose bloom appealed to me, so I stole a number of seeds and brought them home in an almost empty box of sanitary pads.) I have seen Monet's garden in books. Such books are everywhere, certainly in the houses of people who have something of Monet's growing in their garden. The photographs of Giverny (quite different from the paintings) show everything in it to be overgrown, overtall, which is just the kind of garden I like, for I feel that it reveals a comforting generosity of spirit. So it will seem perverse of me to recommend a book of garden paintings not by Monet but by one of his patrons and contemporaries, Gustave Caillebotte. The book, *Caillebotte and His Garden at Yerres,* shows a garden that in feeling is almost the opposite of Giverny. Caillebotte was a well-off man, and his garden has the circumspection of wealth, the order that money can buy. The most evocative painting is of a perfectly aligned row of vegetables under tilted glass cloches, behind two men in bare feet watering what look like heads of lettuce.

I can also recommend packets of seeds from Thompson & Morgan, but only the seeds of plants that would be difficult to find elsewhere. Just for instance, they offer *Meconopsis betonicifolia*, *M. napaulensis*, *M. cambrica* (Welsh poppy), and a really vulgar beauty, *M. cambrica* 'Frances Perry.' Because anything as unusual as *Meconopsis* will be hard to bring to the seedling stage, I suggest that to make a gift like this complete you send the seeds to an agreeable and expert grower who lives not too far from you, so that your plants can be easily picked up and put out for planting in the spring. I have such a person in Jack Manix, of Walker Farm, in Dummerston, Vermont. Last January I sent him twelve different kinds of foxglove seeds I'd bought from Thompson & Morgan, not one of them available through any plantsman that I know of; I picked up the seedlings from Jack in May, planted them in my garden, and look forward to seeing them in bloom next spring.

Among the other things that I would welcome—and so, I imagine, would my fellow gardeners, or at least the gardeners who are at my lowly stage of development—are: tree peonies (to be had from Klehm Nursery); unusual rhododendrons, azaleas, or kalmias (from Mr. Carlson, at Carlson's Gardens, in South Salem, New York); roses, especially old ones, and not the David Austin's and not the modern hybrid tea roses; some terra-cotta pots from the Masini family in Impruneta, Italy; a subscription to *Gardens Illustrated* (of London), the best magazine about gardens being published now; and membership in the Royal Horticultural Society. (This will allow free admission to Wisley, which is useless if you are not living nearby, but the free sub-

scription to the society's magazine, *The Garden,* is the real
benefit, wherever you live.)

If you are reading this with
a gardener in mind and find that
the suggestions for gifts are so
various as to leave you unde-
cided, or are put off by the fact
that roses and peonies are dormant right now and cannot be
shipped until spring, here is
what you can do: draw a picture
of the thing you are planning to
give, put the picture in an enve-
lope, and write the words "To Come" on the outside. It will do very
well. An integral part of a gardener's personality—indeed, a substantial amount of a gardener's world—is made up of the sentiment
expressed by the two words "To Come."

MORE READING

On the day the temperature was 10 degrees below zero, the Ronniger's Seed Potatoes catalogue arrived and that was the cheeriest thing, for I then spent the afternoon sitting in a bathtub of hot water, trying to satisfy a craving for overchilled ginger ale and oranges, and reading this little treasure. It is the most beautiful catalogue I receive each year; it is simple, like a Methodist hymn (I was brought up a Methodist and I am thinking of the first hymn that was in my child's hymnal, "All Things Bright and Beautiful"), plain, straightforward, humble, and comforting—the exact opposite of the White Flower Farm catalogue, which is sumptuous, showy, and expensive-looking. Ronniger's is printed on newsprint, and it has photographs that might have been taken with a not very good camera, or by someone who was not a particularly good photographer, or possibly a combination of the two, but they are adorable, the photographs. They are of people doing something with potatoes, or of machinery used in the cultivation of potatoes, or of potatoes just by themselves, in a bowl or some other kind of household container. It is a catalogue only of potatoes and a few other things that might enhance the flavor of a potato (onions, garlic, salt) or might make a potato grow better (a cover crop of alfalfa or clover). There is a particularly appealing picture of a young boy gathering potatoes; he has a look of blissful concentration on his face, as if the world outside the cultivation of the potato were completely closed to him. But this is only conjecture on my  part; this is only my reading something into a picture I am looking at while sitting in a tub of hot water and drinking cold ginger ale and eating oranges; it could very well be that this boy is deeply familiar not only with the cultivation of the potato but with its history, with the crucial part it played in his ancestors' diet and, therefore, their development as a people.

The process of receiving and reading catalogues may not be as important to my garden as my weeding is, but that is the way I begin the gardening year. Actually, first I despair that there will never be a gardening season again, and then just when that conviction sets in, the seed and plant catalogues start to arrive. The very big, showy ones like the White Flower Farm and Wayside Gardens catalogues are psychological lifts: I never read them; I only look again and again at the pictures. The best catalogues for reading are not altogether unlike wonderful books; they plunge me deep into the world of the garden, the growing of the things advertised (because what are these descriptions of seeds and plants but advertisements), and that feeling of being unable to tear myself away comes over me, and there is that amazing feeling of love, and my imagination takes over as I look out at the garden, which is blanket upon blanket of white, and see it filled with the things described in the catalogue I am reading.

It is in such a state that I read the Ronniger's Seed Potatoes catalogue. Here is a description of that early-maturing potato called the 'Dazoc': "Talk about a delicious red potato . . . we found this one in our neighborhood on the Moyie River Road, grown since 1953 by Bud Behrman, who claims it came from North Dakota and has long since disappeared from commercial markets. Yet, he and his brother have zealously kept it going over the years. Round red deep eyes, excellent flavor, delicious baked and great hash browns, stores well. Bud and family eat them 'til the next crop produces new potatoes." This seemingly straightforward description of a kind of potato provided me with many hours of deliberation and fantasy: How many kinds of early-maturing potatoes can I grow this year? Should 'Dazoc' be among them? Surely a potato grown by someone named Bud Behrman and eaten regularly by him and his family must be a good potato. And the Behrmans—who are the Behrmans? I imagined the Behrman family as the nicest people ever. When I was young and living far away from my family, my life was almost completely empty of domestic routine, and so I made a fetish of the way ordinary people in families lived inside their homes. I read women's magazines obsessively and would often cook entire meals (involving meats in tins and frozen vegetables) from the recipes I found in them. One year I made an entire Thanksgiving dinner that was the same Thanksgiving dinner a family somewhere in the Midwest ate every year. This meal was featured in one of the magazines I read all the time, and the portrayal of these people and their food was so compelling to me that not only did I make the entire meal, but after Sandy Frazier and I ate it, I called up the Midwestern family and told them what I had done; they seemed perplexed and flattered. I then wrote a "Talk" story for *The New Yorker* about the whole episode, which I believe brought to an end that particular expression of alienation in my life. It was the memory of this that made me *not* order the 'Dazoc' potato but remain content with simply imagining the Behrmans and their potato dinners.

Then I moved on to the plantsman Shepherd Ogden and the catalogue he puts out with his wife, *The Cook's Garden*. It is from him that I always get my lettuce and other salad greens, and a beet called 'Formanova,' which he describes this way (the descriptions are written by him; he is an author): "An old favorite of ours, and for good reason. Very tender and sweet, with a unique carrot shape that makes it easy to peel and slice. Can be planted closer than other main crops for high yields." But this beet isn't shaped like a carrot at all, it is shaped like a penis, and I always refer to it that way; I call it the penis-shaped beet. This used to be my favorite catalogue to read before I discovered Ronniger's, and it remains high on the list of the catalogues I go over and over just for the descriptions. I know Shep very well; he had been the previous tenant of the first house I occupied in Vermont, and when I read his catalogue it is quite like talking to him. When I first met him, he mystified me: he is a very tall man who moves much too swiftly for his height and he speaks as swiftly as he moves. Then one day he told me that until he was eighteen years old he was five feet two inches tall and then within a year he grew twelve inches; but all through his teenage years he thought of himself as a short person, and he never got over that. Knowing him in that way, I read his catalogue and feel that he is speaking directly to me.

I am having a minor (I think) infatuation with the Shepherd's Garden Seeds catalogue (no relation to Shep Ogden's catalogue), so I ended up ordering more from them than I meant to. But the description of the 'Kidma' cucumber was hard to resist. "Developed for eating out of hand, they are perfect when picked at 5 to 8 inches long. These cucumbers are not marketed commercially because they are too delicate to stand shipping." This is the luxury of a kitchen garden—growing things you cannot buy at the store. And from Shepherd's Garden Seeds I also got 'Chioggia Striped' beets (described as an Italian variety), which I tried late last summer at a friend's house; they revealed pink-in-white circles when sliced, and they were delicious plain, without a vinaigrette sauce or butter. And I ordered Blue Lake string beans, which I had never grown; they are the most ordinary of string beans to grow, so perversely, for just that reason I wanted to have them this year. On page 38 was a listing for a pink-fleshed potato called 'Cherries Jubilee'; it was described as "luscious" and it is, especially if some of it can be stored over until January for a

dinner of mashed potatoes. My confidence in the Shepherd Seed people increased when I saw that they, too, get their potatoes from Ronniger's, but in the Ronniger's catalogue, 'Cherries Jubilee' is listed in the Samples category, which means you can order only a sample of seeds, each sample weighing one half to one pound. Through Shepherd's I ordered three pounds. But it was in the seeds for flowers that I lost myself: three packets each of 'Old Spice' and 'Early Mammoth' sweet peas. Where I will put them I don't yet know, but they'll all have to go in; there's no such thing as too many sweet peas. I also ordered packets of rose campion, cottage pinks, a foxglove, stock, and double Canterbury bells.

I ordered all these flowers, along with some love-in-a-mist (from Smith & Hawken), daylilies, platycodon, malva, and many other flowers I find beautiful in themselves, completely disregarding Gertrude Jekyll's admonitions about color schemes, complementary or contrasting. Lately, I have been completely immersed in her writing, and it was this extraordinary pleasure that the arrival of the spring catalogues interrupted. In her book *Colour Schemes for the Flower Garden* (which is hard to find in this country; I just happened to come across it in the Borders bookshop in Ann Arbor, Michigan) she says: "I am strongly of opinion that the possession of a quantity of plants, however good the plants may be themselves and however ample their number, does not make a garden; it only makes a *collection*." And again: "Given the same space of ground and the same material, they may either be fashioned into a dream of beauty, a place of perfect rest and refreshment of mind and body—a series of soul-satisfying pictures—a treasure of well-set jewels; or they may be so misused that everything is jarring and displeasing. To learn how to perceive the difference and how to do right is to apprehend gardening as a fine art." All that and much more of what she says about beauty and art in the garden is perfectly true—but what if all the flowers I love and want very much to grow are, when seen together, all wrong, all jarring and displeasing? When I lived in my old house—Mrs. McGovern's house, the Yellow House—and had just started gardening and knew even less than I do now, I decided one day to place a large square bed in the middle of my small lawn. It seemed an odd thing to everybody—everybody told me so—but I just went ahead anyway and put things I liked in this square: white peonies, pink peonies, some yellow lupines, some Johnny-jump-ups, and some portulaca, and then on one edge, lavender and oregano. I found this quadrangle very beautiful and used to sit for long stretches in a chair and gaze at it; at the time I was much in love with lupines.

Devotion to what I love, or *might* love, has caused me to order six *rugosa alba*, a 'Reine des Violettes,' and a 'Madame Isaac Pereire'—all roses—from Wayside Gardens. I wanted four 'Paul's Himalayan Musk' from them also—this is a great pink rambler, which I had planned to run up some old apple trees—an idea not unique to me; I got it from Gertrude Jekyll—but they were all sold out. The rugosa 'Alba' I plan to put in an opening near the road; I don't know how they will look, but they will be full of thorns, so the deer won't eat them; they might even keep the deer out. The 'Reine des Violettes,' too, might be strange—it seemed bluish in the catalogue. I believe I am opposed to blue roses—but once I saw a picture of it I began to imagine it in the corner at the far end of my new stone wall, along with some Canterbury bells, blue and pink platycodon (White Flower Farm), and blue and white campanula. In that large order to White Flower Farm I made—this went against my promise to myself not to order too much from them

because they are expensive and they seem so conceited in their advertisements, but their daylilies are the best I have ever grown—were six
Canada lilies. They look best surrounded by masses of green grass and
brown tree trunks, which is how I saw them when I first fell in love
with them, in a field across from my first house in Vermont, the house
that Shep Ogden used to occupy. They are tall, with thinnish scapes
holding up cadmium-colored, cup-shaped flowers, their heads bent
down as if in intense demonstration of humility. And where to put
these? And then there are two wonderful things from the Jackson &
Perkins catalogue: climbing 'Cécile Brünner' and 'Ballerina' roses. The
'Ballerina' will go at one end of the hollyhocks and the 'Cécile Brünner'
will be at the other end, running up the side of the house and above
the back door and around some windows. I don't know how this will
look. It may not only violate established rules, but also not please me
in the end at all.

In the Park Seed catalogue I saw some beautiful portulaca. When
I think of this little spready plant with short, yet succulent leaves and
rose-like flowers, I think of it by itself, isolated, disregarding how it
might fit into the garden as a whole. My love for this little plant is no
longer a mystery to me. Last summer, as I knelt over it, fretting about
its health (fretting is the most common of all the moods that a gardener can have; a gardener frets even when things are going well), the
origins of my feeling for it became clear to me. When I was little and
lived in Antigua, my mother used to leave me in the care of a woman
who, once we were alone, would take me to visit a friend of hers, a
stevedore, whose name I cannot remember. They would talk for a
while and then disappear together inside—to have sex, I realized some
time later—leaving me all by myself outside. He lived in a small yel-

low house, and the shutters, which they would close when they were inside, were painted a vivid blue. In the front of the house was a little walkway, and on either side of it were two banks carpeted with this flower, portulaca, which we called bachelor's button, and which behaves like a perennial there. These portulaca were crimson and deep purple, and I used to dance up and down around them, pretending that I was a little girl from somewhere else. From that garden I could see the sea, and sometimes a train loaded with sugarcane would pass by, for the house was near the railroad tracks. The woman and I would return to her home, and always she had a bagful of brown sugar, the raw kind, only a stage away from being molasses; she would sometimes give me a lump of it to eat. She and my mother had an enormous fight when my mother found out about our trips to the stevedore's house, but they would have had an enormous fight anyway; people there always do.

Gertrude Jekyll's nurse told her that dandelions were "Nasty Things," and wouldn't allow her to pick them and carry them home. I learned this in a biography of Miss Jekyll written by a woman named Sally Festing, which I read intermittently—in between the spring catalogues and Gertrude Jekyll's own writing. I identify strongly with the pain writers experience when they are criticized, so I don't want to say too loudly how unsatisfying I found this book. It's possible that the nurse's disapproval of dandelions was an event that led to the person Gertrude Jekyll became and her choice of vocation, but the author doesn't say; this kind of speculation doesn't seem to interest her. This book is very decent and discreet—just the qualities I want in a friend, but not in a book I am reading. Was Gertrude Jekyll ever in love with anyone? Did she ever have sex? That's the kind of thing I like to know

about other people. This biography doesn't answer these questions. She had many close friendships with other women, the book does say that. And it says that she knew John Ruskin. But I wanted to know what Gertrude thought of the fact that an English court had annulled Ruskin's marriage, which had never been consummated. Apparently, he had been horrified to discover, on his wedding night, that his wife had pubic hair, she was not smooth and hairless like the nude statues he so admired. (All this I read somewhere else, though.) Festing's biography skips happily along and then, all of a sudden, surprises you with a new piece of information. I carried around in my head the fact that Edwin Lutyens and his wife, Emily, were very much in love, and then, all of a sudden I read that Emily had become involved in some way not clear at all to me with Krishnamurti, and that Edwin turned up at Gertrude's house in the company of Lady Victoria Sackville and her daughter Vita. I guessed that Edwin and Lady Victoria Sackville were having an affair. Sometimes Lutyens called Gertrude Bumps, and sometimes Woozle. She was a very ugly woman and very conscious of it. What better way to divert attention from herself than to make pronouncements about correctness and beauty in the garden. What a perfect example of making a virtue of your own neuroses!

When I finished writing this, the thermometer outside my door read 18 below zero. I now *know* that spring will never come. I shall spend the rest of my life reading seed and plant catalogues, and books about gardens and the people involved with them.

PART II

AN ORDER TO
A FRUIT NURSERY
THROUGH THE MAIL

Please mail to:
Jamaica Kincaid

(DF 127 B) Northern Spy (1)
(DF 114 B) Red Rome (1)
(DF 123 B) Red Stayman Winesap (1) 3 trees @ $15.25 each = $45.75
(DF 604 B) Colette (1)
(DF 610 B) Red Anjou (1)
(DF 602 B) Bartlett (1) 3 trees @ $15.25 each = $45.75
(SF 803 A) Napoleon (1)
(SF 804 A) Schmidt's Bigarreau (1) 2 trees @ $14.75 each = $29.50
(DF 405 A) Santa Rosa (1)
(DF 406 A) Shiro (1) @ $14.75 each = $29.50

(DF 305 A) Hale Haven (1)

(DF 310 A) Red Globe (1) @ $14.75 each = $29.50

(BF 302) Ivanhoe (2) @ $6.15 each = $12.30

(BF 308A) Patriot S.H. @ $6.15 each = $12.30

A total of $204.60

Shipping: $20.40 (Approximately. Please adjust.)

Please charge to my American Express #

Date: 01/94   My telephone number is

I hope this is all clear. If not, do not hesitate to ring me, I would so appreciate it.

This was such a disaster. Only the pear trees are thriving now, and only in the last two years have they flowered.

It isn't easy to grow hard fruits in the garden in my climate and no one told me so; not the catalogue, which succeeded in convincing me that their nursery was situated in a climate even more severe than my own; not my fellow gardeners, who were always serving me a delicious apple pie from their exceptionally productive little orchard—but they had inherited the little orchard from the farmer whose house they had bought. I inherited two apple trees from Dr. Woodworth (a Granny Smith and something else, a red one), but the apples always turn out distorted and crippled-looking, as if someone had assaulted them on purpose when they were tiny; and on top of that, when I cook them, I have to add a lot of sugar just to get a taste sensation of any kind.

It is six years since I sent this order, and after vowing never to order fruit trees through the post again, I am looking at this very same nursery's catalogue and I am making up an order. Oh, please, someone, Help Me!

THE OLD SUITCASE

There was a moment while I was standing inside a tent at the Chelsea Flower Show—a vast, four-day-long display on the grounds of the Royal Hospital in Chelsea, put on by the Royal Horticultural Society every summer—when I experienced a feeling that I imagine the great plant appropriators (David Douglas, Archibald Menzies, Asa Gray, Thomas Nuttall, John Torrey, Joseph Banks, Ernest Wilson) must have experienced upon first seeing a flower of special appeal: I wanted immediately to put the thing I was seeing in my handbag and take it home. I was looking at a *Verbascum* 'Helen Johnson'—a mullein I had never seen before. It was a sport found growing at the Royal Botanic Gardens, at Kew; Helen Johnson is the name of the gardener who found the mullein. Its leaves were just like those of the ordinary wild mullein near my house, which

I have been cultivating, but its flower was a brownish-apricot, almost translucent, with a yellow-and-violet twirl of stamen in the center. Perhaps its appeal for me lay in my not having seen it anywhere before, but I really felt I had to have it. It cannot be propagated by seed, because its seeds are sterile; it can be propagated only through cuttings. I learned this from Adrian Bloom, of Blooms of Bressingham; his was the second stand at which I found *Verbascum* 'Helen Johnson.' While I was speaking to him about this plant, I saw him begin to put some distance—not exactly physical—between us. Familiar as he must be with the fanaticism of people who are involved with plants, my enthusiasm was too much for him. For days after I first saw the 'Helen Johnson' I tramped around the great gardens of England plotting ways to smuggle it back to this country. One day, when I was reading the newspaper, I came across an article about the woes of honey farmers in England. Entire hives have had to be destroyed because they have become infested with bee mite, a parasite that attacks baby bees while they are still in the cell and causes them to be born deformed. It is believed that the bee mite came to England when some beekeepers took their hives to France so the bees could gather lavender pollen there—that while the bees were gathering lavender pollen they picked up the mites, and when they returned to England the mites came with them. I have never, as far as I know, tasted lavender honey, but I wonder if, once it is tasted, it must be tasted again and again, no matter the cost.

Almost as if ashamed of the revulsion and hostility they have for foreign people, the English make up for it by loving and embracing foreign plants wholesale. I am sure there are more plants than people in England originating from the Himalayas. It was at a flower convention, which is what the Chelsea Flower Show is, that I saw this clearly. There was the blue poppy (*Meconopsis betonicifolia*), a flower I had never seen except in a picture; it was everywhere. I thought it might be native to England, but it is not; it comes from the Himalayas and was brought to England by Frank Kingdon-Ward, the plant hunter (that is how he refers to what he was doing; a title of one of his books is *Plant Hunter's Paradise*). I do not know how he died, but I don't believe it was in his own bed.

I was wandering through this place, the Chelsea Flower Show— inside the Great Marquee, where the flowers were on display—a whirl of things forced into perfect bloom, more perfect than anything nature would allow. If I had not known that the Chelsea Flower Show dates back to 1913, I would have thought that this event had never happened before, that this was the first time it had ever been put on. Being there was like being at a child's birthday party. I was in a daze, because I had just gotten off an airplane (it was the middle of the morning, I had already had breakfast, but my body wanted it to be the middle of the night); I was in a daze because I was among so many exquisite flowers and because I was in the midst of people who were so pleasant and kind it was hard to believe they were related to the people who were so rude and insulting to me as I passed through customs. If you ever want to keep up a grudge against someone, don't see that person alongside beautiful flowers. I loved all the people at the Chelsea Flower Show, standing among rhododendrons in impossible shades of mauve, pink, and peach. They came streaming in through an entrance called the Bull-Ring Gate, off the Chelsea Embankment (the same one I had come through), from all directions, as far as I could see, and they looked, not like twentieth-century citizens of a country that used to run the world but like residents of a village—a village far from the city, far even from a town. They displayed the orderliness of the unsophisticated: they lined up; they were polite; they were not nervous; they didn't seem to be expecting (as I was) a terrorist disaster.

The stand of sweet peas was spectacular: none of that 'Mammoth Mixed' or 'Old Spice,' the sparsely flowering varieties common to American gardening (at least the American gardens I know), but large, generous flowers of the clearest, purest, single colors: pure pink, pure white, pure mauve, pure red, with names that seem to have sprung from a mind exhausted with the effort of naming things ('Band-Aid,' 'Royal Wedding').

Just after the sweet peas I came to the place where Peter Beale's roses were being displayed, and a group of people, all twittering and pleasantly agitated, were standing about in the midst of roses that looked even better than the ones in the Wayside Gardens catalogue. Apparently, a duchess had visited; she had unveiled a new rose to the public, and then she had left. When I got there, people were still basking in an "I saw the Duchess" atmosphere. At that moment I realized I had been missing my children, who had stayed home in Vermont with their father. My children like to dress up in some old clothes that used to be mine, clothes that are from the Victorian era, and they pretend that a duchess is coming to tea; she comes, they have tea with her, they quarrel with her, she chops off their heads. This game ends in huge peals of laughter. But my children will grow up and they will stop playing duchess and go on to live, happily or unhappily, the messy lives of ordinary human beings. The best display I saw all day was that of the Crown Estate, a selection of things grown in Windsor Great Park, which belongs to the Queen. The blue poppy was there (a flower nearly impossible to grow here, because of our hot, dry summer); so were some *Hosta sieboldiana.* And there was something there, too, that I had never in my life seen before, something called *Gunnera manicata,* which had leaves so large it seemed as if they could cover ten children's bottoms; the leaves were serrated and deeply cut, like castor-bean leaves. The flowers were about two feet tall, shaped like a pine cone, and emerged from under the leaves, an undelicate and green protuberance. This plant is from Brazil—a very nice man, young, a gardener for the Crown Estate, told me so. I missed the unveiling of the astilbe 'Catherine Deneuve' (Blooms of Bressingham), which is a pink astilbe that looked like many other pink astilbes, but I saw the stoutest, tallest lupines I have ever seen. They were banked up against a wall—a sea of fat, erect whorls covered with red, yellow, orange pea-shaped blooms. And at the Hazeldene Nurseries there was a wonderful display of violas and pansies. Particularly lovely was a cream-colored viola with tiny gray lines running through it, called 'Viola Cream Lady.' As I was walking out of the Great Marquee, I recognized Rosie Atkins, the editor of a beautiful new magazine called *Gardens Illustrated* (I recognized her because there is a photograph of her on the editor's page), and, I suppose, hungry for someone to talk to, I said hello to her and told her how much I liked her magazine (and that is true, I do like it), but I did not tell her that we here in America do not have as good a magazine about gardening as hers, that the closest we come to a good gardening magazine is one called *Fine Gardening*—but who won't approach with caution and suspicion anything with the word "fine" earnestly attached to it?

Outside the tent were gardening tools and furniture—and the show gardens. In a garden called Wildflower and Seaside Garden (it won the Fiskars Sword of Excellence for the best garden at Chelsea that year), burdock was featured prominently, and then and there I began to look forward to the day when I might see a kind of burdock growing in a garden in England and be so filled with longing for it that I would consider, again, breaking the law. And in another show garden I saw the rose 'Rambling Rector' in full bloom, and it made me wish that Peter Beale lived in America, because he sells *real* roses, including this rambler—the kind that would actually survive in the climate I occupy (which, to me, is a real climate). Also, his book about roses is very good, so full of help. It was by now a beautiful afternoon, and I would have plowed on, but I saw something that made me feel like going to my hotel for a rest. To commemorate the hundred-and-fiftieth anniversary of Gertrude Jekyll's birth, the magazine *Country Living* sponsored a garden filled with flowers she liked, and growing more or less in a scheme that the people at the magazine believed she would have approved of. And that was fine, except that they had hired an actress to portray Jekyll, and this woman—wearing Edwardian clothing—made Jekyll look feeble and stingy, as if she had just been removed from a time capsule: damp, full of mildew, not at all like the great artist she was, the great eccentric who always managed, somehow, to deflect close scrutiny. A few days later, in Godalming, Surrey, when I visited Munstead Wood, the house she had Edwin Lutyens build for her, and I was standing in her bedroom, I realized anew how false was that brittle portrayal of her. Everything about the house, with its big rooms, its wide hallway, the specially chosen light wood used for stairs and beams, the wonderful views of woodland and rhododendrons and azaleas and walks and flower beds to be seen from the window, had the texture of sensuality and passion and generosity.

The following morning, before returning to Chelsea, I was reading the newspaper, and after turning away from the extremely unsympathetic opinions of a man with a name (Peregrine Worsthorne) that sounded like an old-fashioned purgative given to children and made from a herb now cultivated only in a physic garden, I came upon an article about a woman who holds the national collection of pelargoniums. She was upset because most people (and until very recently I was one of them) do not know that pelargoniums and geraniums are not the same thing or—to put it coarsely—that geraniums are the ones you can leave outside, while pelargoniums are the ones that must be brought inside, the ones with scented leaves, the ones in window boxes, the ones that turn black when the first frost hits them. She said that before the war (she did not say which war, the British have been involved in many wars, but it is a small country so everyone must know which one "the war" is) people didn't call a pelargonium a geranium, but when the gardeners went away to war the distinction was lost. This, of course, dominated my experience for the rest of the day. If when the gardeners went away, the world of plant differentiation fell apart, what else might have fallen apart? And what did she really mean to say, this woman? If only the world—especially the gardeners—had stayed put? And then I missed my children less, because they always think it's my fault when things don't work out. But there is a big difference between a mother and a gardener.

That day at the flower show, I saw another beautiful grouping of *Verbascum* 'Helen Johnson' at the stand run by Hopleys Plants, and I later read in their catalogue that the nursery had been the first to introduce the flower, in 1991. Barbara Barker, who runs Hopleys with her husband, is a very kind person. She encouraged my enthusiasm, and it was her soothing voice I heard when I read in the catalogue: "We should like to thank all those people who have kindly given us plant material over the years. Do you perhaps have a plant you think we should grow—we would be pleased to swop." This was another lovely day spent among gardeners—gardeners, I kept thinking, who had replaced those who had willy-nilly gone off to war yet who didn't know how to make a new arrangement with the world when the old arrangement no longer worked. Because, also that morning, I had read in yet another newspaper an article by the editor, congratulating himself for having loudly raised the question whether or not the monarchy should be abolished, and to myself I'd thought, People in his position used to help run the world, used to make the heads of millions of people like me spin just by turning a page; now he is reduced to asserting how brave he is for asking a ridiculous question. That evening when a friend called to wish me a happy birthday (I had turned forty-four), I was telling him all this, and he said that once when he was flying over England, he looked down on it and said to himself, God, this looks like the world's oldest suitcase. He did not say what feature in the landscape, architectural or natural, had led him to think that.

No American should go to England without reading Thomas Jefferson. It has become almost impossible for me to think of the two things I like most, history and gardening/botany, without thinking of him, and when I was in England I wanted to visit a garden he had visited. Painshill Park was one of the places he and John Adams went to see on a gardening tour they took together in 1786, while they were negotiating a trade treaty. I learned this from a woman named Eleanor McPeck, who is a garden historian and teaches landscape design at Radcliffe. She had said that, of all the gardens Jefferson saw in England, he liked Painshill Park, in Cobham, Surrey, best. (One of the nice things about hearing her talk about Thomas Jefferson is the way she will say, "Jefferson did this" and "Jefferson was"—this use of his name not implying a phony intimacy but acknowledging that she and he are two citizens on the same public footing.) I am sure it's true that Jefferson loved Painshill, but it is hard to tell this from his own writing. A transcription from his journal reads:

> Painshill—Three hundred and twenty-three acres, garden and park all in one. Well described by Whately. Grotto said to cost £7,000. Whately says one of the bridges is of stone, but both are now of wood, the lower sixty feet high: There is too much evergreen. The dwelling house built by Hopkins, ill-situated: he has not been there in five years: He lived there four years while building the present house. It is not finished: its architecture is incorrect. A Doric Temple, beautiful.

What Thomas Jefferson saw then was the English landscape at its most beautiful, its most manipulated, its most contrived, its most convincing; how vexed and disappointed we become with nature for not actually looking this way. There was a vineyard at Painshill which produced grapes from which wine was made; there was a man-made lake, a Gothic ruin, a mausoleum, a Turkish tent, a grotto, a Temple of Bacchus. Before a courtier named Charles Hamilton imposed order on this landscape, in 1738, it was just brush. After Hamilton, Painshill passed from owner to owner, hand to hand, until the Second World War, when it fell into disrepair and nature reclaimed it. Until twelve years ago, when a trust was created to preserve the site, it had returned to being just brush. It is part of the life of a garden, that because creating a garden is such an act of will, and because (if it is a success) it becomes the place of great beauty which the particular gardener had in mind, the gardener's death (or withdrawal of any kind) is the death of the garden. In a way, a garden is the most useless of creations, the most slippery of creations: it is not like a painting or a piece of sculpture—it won't accrue value as time goes on. Time is its enemy; time passing is merely the countdown for the parting between garden and gardener.

On the day I saw it, Painshill was in the process of being restored. This is a good thing, in its way, but there was also a layer of sadness to it. When I was talking to the people involved in its restoration, they spoke about it in a way that implied it was a part of the national heritage, and I thought that something crucial had been lost over time: the sense of the place not as some sort of national park but as a piece of land a man arranged out of who knows what psychological impulses. I made an observation not original to me, not unlike the one my friend made when he called England an old suitcase: I was in a country whose inhabitants (they call themselves subjects, not citizens) do not know how to live in the present and cannot imagine living in the future, they can live only in the past, because it, the past, has a clear outcome, a winning outcome. A subdued nature is part of this worldview in which everything looks beautiful.

That same afternoon, I saw Munstead Wood. The woman who now lives there (she introduced herself as Lady Clark; I childishly managed to spend the entire time I was there not calling her anything) has installed a swimming pool at the end of Jekyll's old nut walk. She has been criticized for doing this—but why should she have to live in the Gertrude Jekyll House Museum?

There actually is such a thing, a Museum of Garden History, in London. It is in an old church in Lambeth, and in the churchyard there the Tradescants (of *Tradescantia,* or spiderwort), John the Elder and John the Younger, are buried. The Elder was the first real gardener to become a personality in England, and the Younger had been to Virginia for the purpose of bringing plants back to England with him. It was their tomb that I wanted to see, not for any particular reason— just curiosity—but their tomb led me to some other things that are of interest to me. The Tradescants, father and son, are buried together, and the tomb next to theirs holds Captain William Bligh, his wife, his twin sons, and a grandson. There was a small knot garden of dwarf box in the middle of the churchyard, and it is the only knot garden I have ever seen that did not make me feel despair. Inside, in the bookshop, I found a biography of the Tradescants in which the author (Prudence Leith Ross) quotes Francis Bacon as saying: "Nothing is more pleasant to the eye than green grass kept finely shorn," and I could only think to myself that this was someone who never had to cut the grass himself. The exhibition in the museum was about Gertrude Jekyll, again having to do with how long ago she was born. It had everything you would expect: her tools, letters, photographs of her family, and so on—but only two things really interested me. One was Gertrude Jekyll's gardening boots. Anyone who has bought those stupid, uncomfortable clogs or the rubber boots that are advertised in garden catalogues should see these: strong, sensible, and comfortable-seeming leather boots, which were studded on the bottom with iron to make them last. They looked like a well-loved home. The other thing was a copy of her brother Walter's book of songs, which he wrote in tribute to the people of Jamaica. He did not like black people, so naturally, he had to go and live among them. For some people, a fixed state of irritation is oxygen. I understand this all too well.

When I got home myself, I found my pansies committing suicide; they were in desperate need of deadheading. I watched with equal parts of joy and sadness the longest day of the year come and go.

TO NAME IS TO POSSESS

The way you think and feel about gardens and the things growing in them—flowers, vegetables—I can see must depend on where you come from, and I don't mean the difference in opinion and feeling between a person from Spain and a person from England but a difference like this:

The implements of the little feast had been disposed upon the lawn of an old English country-house, in what I should call the perfect middle of a splendid summer afternoon. Part of the afternoon had waned, but much of it was left, and what was left was of the finest and rarest quality. Real dusk would not arrive for many hours; but the flood of summer light had begun to ebb, the air had grown mellow, the shadows were long upon the smooth, dense turf . . . The great still oaks and beeches flung down a shade as dense as that of velvet curtains; and the place was furnished, like a room, with cushioned seats, with rich-coloured rugs, with the books and papers that lay upon the grass.

And this:

The smooth, stoneless drive ran between squat, robust conifers on one side and a blaze of canna lilies burning scarlet and amber on the other. Plants like that belonged to the cities. They had belonged to the pages of my language reader, to the yards of Ben and Betty's uncle in town. Now, having seen it for myself because of my Babamukuru's kindness, I too could think of planting things for merrier reasons than the chore of keeping breath in the body. I wrote it down in my head: I would ask Maiguru for some bulbs and plant a bed of those gay lilies on the homestead. In front of the house. Our home would answer well to being cheered up by such lovely flowers. Bright and cheery, they had been planted for joy. What a strange idea that was. It was a liberation, the first of many that followed from my transition to the mission.

The first quotation is from Henry James's novel *The Portrait of a Lady*, and it can be found isolated in a book called *Pleasures of the Garden: Images from the Metropolitan Museum of Art*, by Mac Griswold, beneath a painting by Pierre Bonnard called *The Terrace at Vernon*.

The painting is rich, rich, rich: rich in color (a profusion of reds, oranges, yellows, blues, greens), rich in material things, rich in bounty from the land. And the quotation itself, with its "little feast," its luxurious observations "splendid summer afternoon" and "flood of summer light," could have been written only by a person who comes from a place where the wealth of the world is like a skin, a natural part of the body, a right, assumed, like having two hands and on them five fingers each.

It is the second quotation that immediately means something to me, especially this: "Bright and cheery, they had been planted for joy. What a strange idea that was." These sentences are from a novel called *Nervous Conditions,* by a woman from Zimbabwe named Tsitsi Dangarembga, and I suppose it is a coming-of-age novel (and really, most people who come from the far parts of the world who write books write at some point about their childhood—I believe it is a coincidence); but the book is also a description of brutality, foreign and local. There are the ingredients for a garden—a plot of land, a hoe, some seeds—but they do not lead to little feasts; they lead to nothing or they lead to work, and not work as an act of self-definition, self-acclaim, but work as torture, work as hell. And so it is quite appropriate that the young narrator—her name is Tambu—finds in the sight of things growing just for the sheer joy of it, liberation.

And what is the relationship between gardening and conquest? Is the conqueror a gardener and the conquered the person who works in the field? The climate of southern Africa is not one that has only recently become hospitable to flowering herbs, and so it is quite possible (most likely) that the ancestors of this girl Tambu would have noticed them and cultivated them, not only for their medicinal value, but also for the sheer joy of seeing them all by themselves in their love-liness, in afternoons that were waning, in light that had begun to ebb. At what moment was this idea lost? At what moment does such ordi-nary, everyday beauty become a luxury?

When the Spanish marauder Hernando Cortez and his army invaded Mexico, they met "floating gardens . . . teeming with flowers and veg-etables, and moving like rafts over the waters"; as they looked down on the valley of Mexico, seeing it for the first time, a "picturesque assem-blage of water, woodland, and cultivated plains, its shining cities and shadowy hills, was spread out like some gay and gorgeous panorama before them," and "stretching far away at their feet were seen noble forests of oak, sycamore, and cedar, and beyond, yellow fields of maize and the towering maguey, intermingled with orchards and blooming gardens"; there were "flowers, which, with their variegated and gaudy colors, form the greatest attraction of our greenhouses"; and again: "Extensive gardens were spread . . . filled with fragrant shrubs and flowers, and especially with medicinal plants. No country has afforded more numerous species of these last . . . and their virtues were per-fectly understood by the Aztecs, with whom medical botany may be said to have been studied as a science." (All this is from *The Conquest of Mexico,* by William H. Prescott, and it is the best history of con-quest I have ever read.) Quite likely, within a generation most of the inhabitants of this place (Mexico), spiritually devastated, would have lost touch with that strange idea—things planted for no other reason than the sheer joy of it.

Certainly if after the conquest an Aztec had gone into a shop and said "It's my husband's birthday. I would like to give him some flowers. May I have a bunch of cocoxochitl, please?" no one would have been able to help her, because cocoxochitl was no longer the name of that flower. It had become the dahlia. In its place of origin (Mexico, Central America), the people who lived there had no dahliamania, no Dahlia Societies, no dinner-plate-size dahlia, no peony-, no anemone-, no ball-shaped-, no water-lily-, no pompon-flowered dahlia. The flower seems to have been appreciated and cultivated for its own sake and for its medicinal value (urinary-tract disorders—cocoxochitl means "water pipes") and as animal fodder. And understandably, beautiful as this flower would have appeared to these people, there were so many other flowers and shrubs and trees and vines, each with some overpowering attribute of shape, height, color of bloom, and scent, that it would not be singled out; the sight of this flower would not have inspired in these people a single criminal act.

At what moment is the germ of possession lodged in the heart? When another Spanish marauder, Vasco Núñez de Balboa, was within sight of the Pacific Ocean, he made his army stay behind him, so that he could be the first person like himself (a European person) to see this ocean; it is likely that could this ocean have been taken up and removed to somewhere else (Spain, Portugal, England), the people for whom it had become a spiritual fixture would long for it and at the same time not even know what it was they were missing. And so the dahlia: Who first saw it and longed for it so deeply that it was removed from the place where it had always been, and transformed (hybridized), and renamed? Hernando Cortez would not have noticed it; to him the dahlia would have been one of the details, a small detail, of something large and grim: conquest. The dahlia went to Europe; it was hybridized by the Swedish botanist Andreas Dahl, after whom it was renamed.

I was once in a garden in the mountains way above Kingston (Jamaica), and from a distance I saw a mass of tall stalks of red flames, something in bloom. It looked familiar, but what it resembled, what it reminded me of, was a flower I cannot stand, and these flowers I saw before me I immediately loved, and they made me feel glad for the millionth time that I am from the West Indies. (This worthless feeling, this bestowing special qualities on yourself because of the beauty of the place you are from, is hard to resist—so hard that people who come from the ugliest place deny that it is ugly at all or simply go out and take someone else's beauty for themselves.) These flowering stalks of red flames turned out to be salvia, but I knew it was salvia only because I had seen it grown— a much shorter variety—in North American gardens; and I realized that I cannot stand it when I see it growing in the north because that shade of red can't be borne well by a dwarfish plant.

I do not know the names of the plants in the place I am from (Antigua). I can identify the hibiscus, but I do not know the name of a white lily that blooms in July, opening at night, perfuming the air with a sweetness that is almost sickening, and closing up at dawn. There is a bush called whitehead bush; it was an important ingredient in the potions my mother and her friends made for their abortions, but I do not know its proper name; this same bush I often had to go and cut down and tie in bunches to make a broom for sweeping our yard; both the abortions and the sweeping of the yard, actions deep and shallow, in a place like that (Antigua) would fall into the category called Household Management. I had wanted to see the garden in Kingston so that I could learn the names of some flowers in the West Indies, but along with the salvia the garden had in it only roses and a single anemic-looking yellow lupine (and this surprised me, because lupine is a temperate zone flower and I had very recently seen it in bloom along the roadside of a town in Finland).

This ignorance of the botany of the place I am from (and am of) really only reflects the fact that when I lived there, I was of the conquered class and living in a conquered place; a principle of this condition is that nothing about you is of any interest unless the conqueror deems it so. For instance, there was a botanical garden not far from where I lived, and in it were plants from various parts of the then British Empire, places that had the same climate as my own; but as I remember, none of the plants were native to Antigua. The rubber tree from Malaysia (or somewhere) is memorable because in the year my father and I were sick at the same time (he with heart disease, I with hookworms), we would go and sit under this tree after we ate our lunch, and under this tree he would tell me about his parents, who had abandoned him and gone off to build the Panama Canal (though of course he disguised the brutality of this). The bamboo grove is memorable because it was there I used to meet people I was in love with. The botanical garden reinforced for me how powerful were the people who had conquered me; they could bring to me the botany of the world they owned. It wouldn't at all surprise me to learn that in Malaysia (or somewhere) was a botanical garden with no plants native to that place.

There was a day not long ago when I realized with a certain amount of bitterness that I was in my garden, a flower garden, a garden planted only because I wished to have such a thing, and that I knew how I wanted it to look and knew the name, proper and common, of each thing growing in it. In the place I am from, I would have been a picture of shame: a woman covered with dirt, smelling of manure, her hair flecked with white dust (powdered lime), her body a cauldron of smells pleasing to her, and her back crooked with pain from bending over. In the place I am from, I would not have allowed a man with the same description as such a woman to kiss me.

It is understandable that a man like Andreas Dahl would not have demurred at his eponymous honor, because this was the eighteenth century and the honor was bestowed on him by a king (a Charles of Spain, who might well have named the flower after himself, or a close relative, or any one of the many henchmen in his service). Andreas Dahl was very familiar with the habit of naming, for he had been a pupil of Carlolus Linnaeus. This man, Carlolus Linnaeus, had been a botanist and a doctor, and that made sense, botanist and doctor: they went together because plants were the main source of medicine in that part of the world then, as was true in the other parts of the world then also. From Sweden (his place of origin) he had gone to the Netherlands for his doctor's degree, and it was there, while serving as personal physician to a rich man, that he worked out his system (binomial) of naming plants. The rich man (his name was George Clifford) had four greenhouses filled with plants not native to the Netherlands—not native to Europe at all but native to the places that had been recently conquered. *The Oxford Companion to Gardens* (a book I often want to hurl across the room, it is so full of prejudice) describes Linnaeus as "enraptured" with seeing all these plants from far away, because his native Sweden did not have anything like them, but most likely what

happened was that he saw an opportunity, and it was this: These countries in Europe shared the same botany, more or less, but each place
called the same thing by a different name; and these people who make
up Europe were (are) so contentious anyway, they would not have
agreed to one system for all the plants they had in common, but these
new plants from far away, like the people far away, had no history, no
names, and so they could be given names. And who was there to dis-
pute Linnaeus, even if there was someone who would listen?

 This naming of things is so crucial to possession—a spiritual pad-
lock with the key thrown irretrievably away—that it is a murder, an
erasing, and it is not surprising that when people have felt themselves
prey to it (conquest), among their first acts of liberation is to change
their names (Rhodesia to Zimbabwe, LeRoi Jones to Amiri Baraka).
That the great misery and much smaller joy of existence remain
unchanged no matter what anything is called never checks the
impulse to reach back and reclaim a loss, to try and make what happened look as if it had not happened at all.

 As I started to write this (at the very beginning) I was sitting at a
window that looked out over my own garden, a new one (I have just
moved to this place), and my eye began in the deep-shade area, where
I had planted some astilbe and hosta and *Ranunculus repens,* and I
thought how beautifully the leaves of the astilbe went with the leaves
of the ranunculus, and I took pleasure in that, because in putting
things together (plants) you never really know how it will all work until
they do something, like bloom. (It will be two or three years before I
know whether the clematis really will run up the rosebushes and
bloom together with them and whether it will really look the way I
have imagined.) Just now the leaves in the shade bed are all comple-

mentary (but not in a predictable way—in a way I had not expected, a thrilling way). And I thought how I had crossed a line; but at whose expense? I cannot begin to look, because what if it is someone I know? I have joined the conquering class: who else could afford this garden—a garden in which I grow things that it would be much cheaper to buy at the store?

My feet are (so to speak) in two worlds, I was thinking as I looked farther into the garden and saw, beyond the pumpkin patch, a fox emerge from the hedge—the same spot in the hedge where I have seen the rabbits and a family of malicious woodchucks emerge (the woodchucks to eat not the lettuce or the beans or the other things I would expect them to eat but the tender new shoots and tendrils of the squash vines). The fox crossed the garden and ran behind the shed, and I could see him clearly, his face a set of sharp angles, his cheeks planed, his body a fabric of tightly woven gray and silver hair over a taut frame of sinew and bones, his tail a perfect furpiece. He disappeared into the opposite hedge and field; he, too, had the look of the marauder, wandering around hedge and field looking for prey. That night, lying in my bed, I heard from beyond the hedge where he had emerged sounds of incredible agony; he must have found his prey; but the fox is in nature, and in nature things work that way.

I am not in nature. I do not find the world furnished like a room, with cushioned seats and rich-colored rugs. To me, the world is cracked, unwhole, not pure, accidental; and the idea of moments of joy for no reason is very strange.

MONET'S GARDEN

What would the garden be without the paintings? Would I be standing in it (the garden, Claude Monet's garden), looking at the leaf-green arches on which were trained roses ('American Pillar,' 'Dainty Bess,' 'Paul's Scarlet Rambler') and clematis ('Montana Rubens'), looking at the beds of opium poppies, Oriental poppies, looking at the sweep of bearded iris (they had just passed bloom), looking at dottings of fat peonies (plants only, they had just passed bloom), and looking at roses again, this time standardized, in bloom in that way of the paintings (the real made to shimmer as if it will vanish from itself, the real made to seem so nearby and at the same time so far away)?

It was June. I was standing looking at the solanum 'Optical Illusion' (Monet himself grew the species *Solanum retonii* but solanum 'Optical Illusion' is what I saw on a label placed next to this plant) and the hollyhock 'Zebrina' (they were in bloom in all their simple straightforwardness, their uncomplicated mauve-colored petals streaked with lines of purple, and this color purple seemed innocent of doubt); looking at the other kind of hollyhock, *rosea,* which was only in bud, so I could not surreptitiously filch the seedpods; looking at the yellow-flowering thalictrum, the poppies again (only this time they were field poppies, *Papaver rhoeas,* and they were in a small area to the side of the arches of roses, but you can't count on them being there from year to year, for all the poppies sow themselves wherever they want); looking at an area of lawn set off by apple trees trained severely along a fence made of wire painted green and beech posts.

I was looking at all these things, but I had their counterparts in Monet's paintings in my mind. It was June, so I had missed the lawn full of blooming daffodils and fritillarias, they came in the spring. And all this was only the main part of the garden, separate from the water garden, famous for the water lilies, the wisteria growing over the Japanese bridge, the Hoschedé girls in a boat.

And would the water garden be the same without the paintings? On the day (days) I saw it, the water garden—that is, the pond with lilies growing in it—the Hoschedé girls were not standing in a boat on the pond, for they have been dead for a very long time now, and if I expected them to appear standing in the boat, it is only because the pond itself looked so familiar, like the paintings, shimmering (that is sight), enigmatic (that is feeling, or what you say about feeling when you mean many things), and new (which is what you say about something you have no words for yet, good or bad, accept or reject: "It's new!")—yes, yes, so familiar from the paintings.

But when I saw the water garden itself (the real thing, the thing that Monet himself had first made and the thing that has become only a memory of what he had made after he was no longer there to care about it, he had been dead a long time by then), it had been restored and looked without doubt like the thing Monet had made, a small body of water manipulated by him, its direction coming from a natural source, a nearby stream. On the day I saw it, the pond, the Hoschedé girls (all three of them) were not in a boat looking so real that when they were seen in that particular painting (*The Boat at Giverny*) they would then define reality. The Hoschedé girls were not there, for they had long been dead also, and in fact, there were no girls in a boat on the pond, only a woman, and she was in a boat and holding a long-handled sieve, skimming debris from the surface of the pond. The pond itself (and this still is on the day that I saw it) was in some flux, water was coming in or water was going out, I could not really tell (and I did not really want to know). The water lilies were lying on their sides, their roots exposed to clear air, but on seeing them that way I immediately put them back in the arrangement I am most familiar with them in the paintings, sitting in the water that is the canvas with all their beginnings and all their ends hidden from me. The wisteria growing over the Japanese bridge was so familiar to me (again), and how very unprepared I was to see that its trunk had rotted out and was hollow and looked ravaged, and ravaged is not what Monet evokes in anyone looking at anything associated with him (even in the painting he made of Camille, his wife before Alice, dead, she does not look ravaged, only dead, as if to be dead is only another way to exist). But to see these things—the wisteria, the Japanese bridge, the water lilies, the pond itself (especially the pond, for here the pond looks like a canvas)—is to be suddenly in a whirl of feelings. For here is the real thing, the real material thing: wisteria, water lily, pond, Japanese bridge—in its proper setting, a made-up landscape in Giverny, made up by the gardener Claude Monet. And yet I see these scenes now because I had seen them the day before in a museum (the Musée d'Orsay) and the day before that in another museum (the Musée Marmottan) and many days and many nights (while lying in bed) before that, in books, and it

is the impression of them (wisteria, water lily, pond, Japanese bridge) that I had seen in these other ways before (the paintings in the museums, the reproductions in the books) that gave them a life, a meaning outside the ordinary.

A garden will die with its owner, a garden will die with the death of the person who made it. I had this realization one day while walking around in the great (and even worthwhile) effort that is Sissinghurst, the garden made by Vita Sackville-West and her husband, Harold Nicolson. Sissinghurst is extraordinary: it has all the impersonal beauty of a park (small), yet each part of it has the intimacy of a garden—a garden you could imagine creating yourself if only you were so capable. And then again to see how a garden will die with the gardener, you have only to look at Monet's friend and patron Gustave Caillebotte; the garden he made at Petit Gennevilliers no longer exists; the garden in Yerres, where he grew up, the one depicted in some of his paintings, is mostly in disarray. When I saw the potagerie, the scene that is the painting *Yerres, in the Kitchen Garden: Gardeners Watering the Plants* was now a dilapidated forest of weeds: a cat who looked as if it belonged to no one stared crossly at me; a large tin drum stood just where you might expect to see a gardener, barefoot and carrying two watering cans. The Yerres River itself no longer seemed wide and deep and mysteriously shimmering (as in *Boater Pulling In his Périssoire, Banks of the Yerres* or *Bathers, Banks of the Yerres*), it was now only ordinarily meandering, dirty, like any old memory.

And so, would the garden, in Giverny, in which I was standing one day in early June, mean so much to me and all the other people traipsing around without the paintings? The painting *The Artist's*

Garden at Giverny is in a museum in Connecticut, the painting *The Flowering Arches* is in a museum in Arizona, the painting *The Japanese Footbridge* is in a museum in Houston, *Water Lilies* are everywhere. On seeing them, these paintings, either in the setting of a museum or reproduced in a book, this gardener can't help but long to see the place they came from, the place that held the roses growing up arches, the pond in which the lilies grew, the great big path (called the Grand Allée) that led from the front door of the house and divided the garden in two, the weeping willow, the Japanese bridge, the gladiolas (they were not yet in bloom when I was there), the peonies (they were past bloom when I was there), the dahlias (they were not yet in bloom when I was there).

That very same garden that he (Monet) made does not exist; that garden died, too, the way gardens do when their creators and sustainers disappear. And yet the garden at Giverny that he (Monet) made is alive in the paintings, and the person seeing the paintings (and that would be anyone, really) can't help but wonder where they came from, what the things in the painting were really like in their vegetable and animal (physical) form. In the narrative that we are in (the Western one), the word comes before the picture; the word makes us long for a picture, the word is never enough for the thing just seen—the picture!

The garden that Monet made has been restored to itself, has been restored so that when we now look at it, there is no discrepancy, it is just the way we remember it (but this must be the paintings), it is just the way it should be. As I was standing there in June (nearby were tray upon tray of ageratum seedlings about to be planted out in a bedding), a man holding a camera (and he was the very definition of confidence) said to me, "Monet knew exactly what he was doing." I did not say to him that people who know exactly what they are doing always end up with exactly what they are doing.

The house at Giverny in which he (Monet) lived has also been restored. It can be seen, a tour of the house and garden is available. As I was going through the rooms of the house—the yellow dining room, the blue kitchen, the bedrooms with the beds all properly made up, the drawing room with prints of scenes and people from Japan—I hurried, I rushed through. I felt as if at any moment now, the occupant, the owner (Monet, whoever it might be) would return and I would be caught looking into someone's private life. I would be caught in a place I was not really meant to be.

WHAT JOSEPH BANKS

WROUGHT

Whatever it is in the character of the English people that leads them to obsessively order and shape their landscape and to such a degree that it, the English landscape, looks like a painting (tamed, framed, captured, kind, decent, good, pretty)—and a painting never looks like it, the English landscape, unless it is a bad painting—this quality of character that leads to obsessive order and shape in the landscape is blissfully lacking in the Antiguan people. I make this unfair comparison (unfair to the Antiguan people? unfair to the English people? I cannot tell, but there is an unfairness here somewhere) only because so much of the character of the Antiguan people is influenced by and directly inherited (through conquest) from the English people; I can cite immediately the pity and cruelty showered at once on the weak, and a love of gossip (which I think is one reason the English people have produced such great novelists, but this has not yet worked to the advantage of the Antiguan people).

When the English were a presence in Antigua, the places they lived in were surrounded by severely trimmed hedges of plumbago, topiaries of willow (casuarina), frangipani, hibiscus; their grass was green (strange, because water was scarce) and freshly cut; there were arches covered with roses, and there were beds of marigolds and cannas and chrysanthemums. Ordinary Antiguans then (and by "ordinary Antiguans" I mean the Antiguan people who are descended from the African slaves brought to this island by Europeans; this turns out to be not an uncommon way to become ordinary), the ones who had some money and so could live in a house with more than one room, had gardens in which only flowers were grown, and this would make even more clear that they had some money, because all their outside space was not devoted only to feeding their families but also to the sheer beauty of things. I can remember in particular one such family who lived in a house with many rooms (four to be exact) and they had a lawn always neatly cut and they had beds of flowers, though I can now remember only roses and marigolds, and I can remember this because once I was sent to get a bouquet of roses for my godmother on her birthday; and this family also had in the middle of their small lawn a casuarina tree pruned so that it took the shape of a pine tree (pyramidal), and at Christmas time this tree was decorated with colored lightbulbs (which was so unusual and luxurious to me that when I passed by this house at that time I would beg to be allowed to stop and stare at it for a while). At Christmas time the willow tree would suddenly be called a Christmas tree, and for a time when my family must have had some money (it would have been only a small amount) I had a Christmas tree, a lonely spindly branch of a willow tree sitting in a bucket of water in our very small house, though no one in my family, and I am almost certain no one in the family of the people with the lighted-up willow tree, had any idea of the origins of the tradition of the Christmas tree and the things associated with it.

When these people (the Antiguans) lived under the influence of those other people (the English) there was naturally an attempt among certain of them to imitate their rulers in this particular way, arranging a landscape, and they did this without question; they can't be faulted for not asking what it was they were doing, that is the way these things work. The English left, and their landscaping influence went with them. The Americans came, but Americans are not interested in influencing people directly; Americans instinctively understand the childlike principle of monkey see, monkey do, and at the same time they are more divided, more complicated than the English. Americans behave like this: half of them believe in and support strongly a bad thing their government is doing; the other half do not believe in and protest strongly a bad thing their government is doing. The bad thing succeeds and everyone, protester and supporter alike, immensely enjoys the results of the bad thing. This division in the many is startling in the individual. Thomas Jefferson, the third American President and a great gardener in his time, owned slaves and strongly supported the idea of an expanded American Territory, which meant the demise of the people who owned and lived on this land. At the same time, he passionately advocated ideas about freedom, ideas that the descendants of the slaves and the people who were defeated and robbed could use in defense of themselves (the guns they would have were not powerful enough). He was an advocate of the great trek his former secretary, the land adventurer and botany thief Meriwether Lewis, made through the West. The Lewisia, the state flower of Montana, is named after him; Clarkia, not a flower of any state as far as I know, is named for his co-adventurer and botany thief, William Clark.

What did the botanical life of Antigua consist of at the time another famous adventurer (Christopher Columbus) first saw it? To see a garden in Antigua now will not supply a clue. The bougainvillea (named for another restless European, the sea adventurer Louis de Bougainville, the first Frenchman to cross the Pacific) is native to tropical South America; the plumbago is from southern Africa; the croton is from Malaysia; the hibiscus is from Asia (unfringed petal) and East Africa (fringed petal); the allamanda is from Brazil; the poinsettia (named for an American ambassador, Joseph Poinsett) is from Mexico; the bird of paradise is from southern Africa; the Bermuda lily is from Japan; the flamboyant tree is from Madagascar; the casuarina comes from Australia; the Norfolk pine comes from Norfolk Island in the South Pacific; the tamarind tree is from Africa and Asia. The mango is from Asia. The breadfruit is from the East Indies. This food, the breadfruit, has been the cause of more disagreement between parents and their children than anything I can think of. No West Indian that I know has ever liked it. It was sent to the West Indies by Joseph Banks, the English naturalist and world traveler, and the founder of Kew Gardens, which was then a clearinghouse for all the plants stolen from the various parts of the world these people had been (the climbing rose *R. banksiae* from China was named for his wife). He sent tea to India, he sent the West Indies the breadfruit; it was meant to be a

cheap food for feeding slaves. It was in the cargo that Captain Bligh
was carrying to the West Indies on the *Bounty* when his crew so correctly mutinied. (Perhaps Antiguan children sense intuitively the part
this food has played in the history of injustice and so they will not eat

it.) It grows readily, it bears fruit abundantly, it is impervious to drought, a serious impediment to the growing of things anywhere. In a place like Antigua the breadfruit is not a food, it is a weapon.

What herb of any beauty grew in this place? What tree? And did the people who lived there grow them for their own sake? I do not know, I can find no record of it. I can only make a guess in this way: the frangipani, the mahogany tree, the cedar tree are all native to the West Indies, and Antigua is in the West Indies. The botany of Antigua exists in medicinal folklore. My mother and I were sitting on the steps in front of her house one day and I suddenly saw a beautiful (to me now; when I was a child I thought it ugly) bush whose fruit I remembered playing with when I was a child; it is a herbacious plant with a red stem covered with red thorns, and emerald-green simple leaves with the same red thorns running down the leaf from the leaf stalk. I cannot remember what its flowers looked like—it was not in flower when I saw it while I was sitting with my mother—but its fruit is a small, almost transparent red berry, and it is with this I used to play. We children sometimes called it chinaberry; because of its transparent, glassy look, it reminded us of china dinnerware (we were only vaguely familiar with such a thing as china, having seen it perhaps once or twice) and sometimes baby tomato—because of its size and to show that it was not real, a baby anything was not a real thing. When I pointed it out to my mother, she called it something else; she called it cancanberry bush and said that years ago when people could not afford to see doctors, if their child had thrush, they would make a paste with this fruit and rub it inside the child's mouth, and this would make it go away. But, she said, no one bothers with any of this anymore. The day before that, a friend of hers had come to pay her a visit, and when my mother offered her friend something to eat and drink, her friend declined because, she said, she had some six sixty-six and maiden-blush tea waiting at home for her. This tea is taken on an empty stomach, and it is used for all sorts of ailments, including abortions. I have never seen six sixty-six in flower, but its leaves are a beautiful ovoid shape and a deep green, qualities that are of value in a garden devoted to the shape and color of leaves.

Whenever I say to someone that there is a relationship between gardening and prosperity, they are apt to throw in my face the image of that oppressed, sad, pinched-face person, the English cottage gardener. Apart from the fact that the person who usually says this to me is usually someone who does not know a cottage gardener personally and would never be a friend of one, the fact is that a cottage gardener is not a gardener any more than my mother is a gardener. My mother is someone who puts a few things here and there for her own use; the beauty or not-beauty of it, she decides. And if the cottage gardener does not exist in a place like Antigua, it is because people from places like Antigua are not called things like that; casual botanical conversation, the Latin names for plants, a discussion of the binomial system— where I am from, I am not aware that an atmosphere for these things exists in this place. I can remember well the cruel English person who was my botany teacher and that, in spite of her cruelty, botany and history were my favorite subjects in school. With this in mind, I visited a bookstore (the only bookstore in Antigua) to see what texts were now being used in the schools and to see how they compared with what was taught to me then; the botany I had studied was the botany of the British Empire in Africa and Asia, some of the very same plants that are now widely cultivated in Antigua and must seem to most

Antiguans (if they ever think about it) as typical of their native land-scape. But botany as a subject is no longer taught in Antiguan schools; the study of plants is now called Agriculture. Perhaps this is a more realistic view, because the awe and poetry of botany cannot be eaten, the mystery and beauty in the knowledge of botany cannot be taken to market.

And yet the people on Antigua have a relationship to agriculture that cannot please them at all. Their very presence on this island hundreds of years ago has to do with this thing, agriculture. When they (we) were brought to this island from Africa a few hundred years ago, it was not for their pottery-making skills or for their way with a loom; it was for the free labor they could provide in the fields. In an account of her life, Mary Prince, an enslaved African woman who spent some time as a slave in Antigua, wrote:

My master and mistress went on one occasion into the country, to Date Hill, for change of air, and carried me with them to take charge of the children, and to do the work of the house. While I was in the country, I saw how the field negroes are worked in Antigua. They are worked very hard and fed but scantily. They are called out to work before day-break, and come home after dark; and then each has to heave his bundle of grass for the cattle pen. Then on Sunday morning, each slave has to go out and gather a large bundle of grass; and, when they bring it home, they have all to sit at the manager's door and wait till he come out: often they have to wait there till past eleven o'clock, without any breakfast. After that, those that have yams or potatoes, or fire-wood to sell, hasten to market to buy salt fish or pork, which is a great treat for them.

It seems so clear to me, then, that a group of people who have had such a horrible historical association with growing things would try to make any relationship to it dignified (agriculture) and useful.

In a book I am looking at (even to read it is to look at it, the type is as big as a doll's teacup), called *The Tropical Garden,* I find sentences like: "The concept of a private garden planted purely for aesthetic purposes was generally alien to tropical countries" and "There was no tradition of ornamental horticulture among the inhabitants of most hot weather places. Around the average home there might be a few specimens chosen especially because of their scented flowers or because they were believed to bring good fortune . . . Nor would much, if any, attention be paid to attractive landscape design in such gardens: early accounts by travelers in the tropics abound in enthusiastic descriptions of jungle scenery, but a reader will search in vain for one praising the tasteful arrangement of massed ornamental beds and contrasting lawns of well-trimmed grass around the homes of natives." And what can I say to that? No doubt it is true. And no doubt also, contrasting lawns and massed ornamental beds are signs of something, and I want to say what that something is: someone has been humbled, someone is on his knees wondering what happened, someone will have an eternal love of concrete. Just to show what I mean: on page 62 of this book is a photograph of eight men, natives of India, pulling a heavy piece of machinery used in the upkeep of lawns. They are without shoes. They are wearing the clothing of schoolboys, khaki shorts and khaki short-sleeved shirts. A look of bliss is not on their faces. The caption for this photograph reads: "Shortage of labour was never a problem in the maintenance of European features in large colonial gardens; here a team of workers is shown rolling a lawn at the Gymkhana Club in Bombay."

And here is another question the author, Mr. Warren, might have asked himself: What if the people living in the tropics, the ones whose history isn't tied up with and contaminated by slavery and indenturedness, are content with their surroundings, are happy to observe an invisible hand at work and from time to time laugh at some of the ugly choices this hand makes, have more important things to do than making a small tree large, a large tree small, a tree whose blooms are usually yellow, black; what if these people are not spiritually feverish, restless, and full of envy? I don't have an answer to these questions myself; if I did I would tell.

There must be many ways to have someone be the way you would like them to be; I only know of two with any certainty: You can hold a gun to their head or you can clearly set out before them the thing you would like them to be, and eventually they admire it so much, without even knowing they do so, that they adopt your ways, almost to the point of sickness; they come to believe that your way is their way and would die before they give it up. When I was looking at the book of tropical gardens, the flowers and the trees so familiar to me from my childhood, so native to a background like mine, were without any hold at all on me. I do not really like the bougainvillea, I do not really like the hibiscus. The corallita (from Mexico), so beautiful when tended, so ugly when left to itself, making everything it comes near look rusty and shabby, is not a plant I like at all. I returned from a visit to Antigua, the place where I was born, to a small village in Vermont, the place where I choose to live. It was spring then. The tulips I had planted last autumn were in bloom and I liked sitting caressing their petals, which felt like skin made up of peau de soie, deliciously disgusting. The dizzy-making yellow of dandelions and marsh marigolds were in fields and riverbanks and marshes. I like these things. I do not like daffodils, but that's a legacy of the gun-to-the-head approach, for I was forced to memorize the poem by William Wordsworth when I was a child. I transplanted my foxgloves to a place in the middle of a grove of pine trees. I waited for the things I had ordered in the deep cold of winter to come. They started to come. Mr. Pembroke, who represents our village in the Vermont legislature, came and helped me dig some of the holes where some of the things I wanted were to be planted. Mr. Pembroke is a very nice man, there is not a look of misery on his face, on his face is a look of ordinary human something, but exactly what I do not know. We agree on a price, he sends me a bill. The days are growing longer and longer, and then they'll get shorter again. I am now used to that, I love that. There is no order in my garden. I live in America now. Americans are too impatient with memory, one of the things order thrives on.

THE GLASSHOUSE

The botanical garden that I knew as a child did not need a glass enclosure. The atmosphere in which it was situated, a hot, humid climate, provided that. To us, it was an unusual idea: a garden in which were gathered specimens of plants from various parts of the British Empire; but we soon absorbed it, got used to it, took it for granted, the way we had with another European idea, that of leaving your own native (European) climate and living in places native to other people whom you cannot stand. Again, it was an unusual idea and we associated it with our dominators, the English people, their love, their need to isolate, name, objectify, possess various parts, people, and things in the world.

This botanical garden of my childhood is an enormous expanse of land, Edenic, in my memory. For a large period of my childhood life, I spent every Sunday afternoon there; for a shorter period of my child-hood life, when my father and I were happily (it seems to me now) sick together, he with heart and digestive problems, me with a persistent case of hookworm, I spent many weekday afternoons there. On Sunday afternoons I could never seem to traverse the whole of it. I was always surprised when the dark of nighttime began to come on and I was still in only one part of it, the part of it that I had headed for the minute I entered.

The parts of that botanical garden that were my destination on Sunday afternoons were the secluded parts. The Bamboo Grove (it was called that, the Bamboo Grove) was particularly favored. It was there in the middle of this patch of giant grasses, a species of plant completely foreign to Antigua, that I met the great loves of my then life. These great loves were all girls; for them to have been boys would have been a serious mistake, a mistake that would have, not might have, changed my life, for I knew either by instinct, or it had been drummed into me, that boys (who eventually grow into men) never think of consequences, never care about consequences unless it pleases them to do so, never indulge in the fantasies of pretending, and so must take everything to its logical conclusion, at which point they then move to take on another event and bring it to its logical con-clusion.

What type of bamboo was in the Bamboo Grove, where it was from, I do not now remember. I am sure it had some little legend of information placed near it, because not only is such a thing expected, it is also just the sort of thing the people planting the bamboo in its botanical context would do. It is not native to the place I am from. This clump of bamboo that I knew, the only clump of bamboo that I knew then, could have come from that mysterious place known to me as the Far East, or that mysterious place known to me as Africa. The one thing I do know is that the bamboo was brought to me by people I was most familiar with, people who had influenced me to such a degree that though I did not resemble them in any physical way, I thought of myself as more like them than the people I did resemble in a physical way.

There was a rubber tree. Did I know that its proper name was *Ficus elastica?* I doubt it; in any case, this would not have interested me. I knew it was a part of the economy of some of the people of the mysterious Far East. The people native to the Far East, like the people native to everywhere, were workers; that is, they worked in the fields where they cultivated the plants native to their place or the plants that had been made native to their place.

There was a rubber tree in this botanical garden. It was not too far away from the grove of bamboo. The rubber tree was a massive twist of trunks and roots all coiled up and turned in and out of each other. When first seen by any of us (and by us, I mean not only my immediate family but the people of my small island), it was a curiosity; eventually we accepted its presence in our midst, even as we accepted our own presence in our midst, for we, too, were not native to the place we were in. Did I know that such a gigantic tree could be epiphytic? And should knowing that have been consoling? The man who was not really my father, I only thought him so, he was presented to me as that, my father, he and I were once sick at the same time, he with problems in his chest and stomach that had been diagnosed as a malfunctioning heart and a malfunctioning digestive tract; I with a severe and persistent case of hookworm. In a poor country his maladies had no real cure from a doctor; in a poor country parasites of every kind, except the human kind, the colonial, that severe and persistent problem, are attacked zealously, and their (the parasites who are not human) eradication is the goal of every good person.

When my father and I grew sick simultaneously, we had a delicious time. We had not meant to. In the mornings, after our breakfast of porridge and eggs and grapefruit, we would lie in bed with our feet resting on the windowsill; the sun, by some strange arrangement, never came in to make the inside of our small house hot, it always remained just outside the doorway, just at the windowsill. While we were lying in bed, my father obsessively studied football coupons, hoping to settle on a combination of English football teams that would all do the same thing (I can't remember whether it was that they would all win or they would all lose), and if he chose correctly, he would win a great deal of money. He never managed to choose correctly. I read a book, any book, I can't remember now what they would have been, but it was something of which my mother had a high opinion. After our lunch, which would have been something delicious, but something I am sure (even now) I did not eat much of, my father and I would set out on a walk. Our destination was always the botanical garden, and in the botanical garden our destination would eventually be a nice afternoon spent sitting under the rubber tree.

The reason why when we reached the botanical garden our destination would eventually be the rubber tree was that my father would first make stops in various sections of the garden and surreptitiously pick parts of other plants growing there, from which he would make a tea to treat his ailments. There was one shrub in particular, called by him a myrtle bush. It was a low-growing shrub, with small thorns down its long, slightly drooping stems, and it bore fruit, small red berries. I do not remember seeing it in flower. There were other plants that he felt compelled to pick to treat his illnesses, but I do not remember them as clearly as I do this myrtle bush, which now I see resembles a barberry (and perhaps this whole episode explains my resistance to barberries and why I do not have them growing in my garden; on the other hand, were I to have a passion for barberries, this whole episode could explain it, too). His making of a tea from this bush was an unusual sight, for my father was never seen performing any task that was vaguely domestic. He did not even polish his own shoes, my mother did that; she even made sure he had a fresh glass of water each night in which to place his two rows of false teeth (the false teeth, she felt sure, were the cause of his digestive problems).

It was in the shade of the distorted branches of the rubber tree (though this distortion is perfectly natural to the rubber tree) in the botanical garden of St. John's, Antigua, a garden that was the creation of the most ambivalent of people, that I came to know important things, though I came to understand them only long after. Not the least of them is how I became a writer, or at least some of the things that have contributed to my becoming a writer. My father: his mother left him when he was a small child, small enough for it to matter so much to him that he still spoke of it when he was over fifty years old, but of course it turns out that no matter what time your mother leaves you, it always matters; she went to England and he never saw her again. She once sent him a pair of shoes, but they were too big and they were put away; when he tried them on again, he had outgrown them. Perhaps at the same time, perhaps before, perhaps afterward (it was never made clear to me) his father left him and went off to build the Panama Canal. If my father knew then that his own father had not single-handedly built the Panama Canal, he did not make it clear to me. It wasn't until much later, when I met other people from the West Indies who all had stories of their own father's going off to build the Panama Canal, that I came to feel this: it is possible that, in a way, a very human way, my father, when sitting under the rubber tree in the botanical garden, was in the presence, the atmosphere, the shrine of Possession, and that he himself was an object, a mere thing, within it. The rubber tree was not present in Antigua through a benign curiosity; the Antigua that he lived in had not come about through the catastrophe common to the uncaring and uneven acts of nature. My father had absorbed all this culture of Possession: the rubber tree, the bamboo tree, the plant from which his medicine was made (this shrub was not native to Antigua, I do not know where it is from, but I have never seen it anywhere but in the botanical garden), the bamboo grove, all that was in the botanical garden, including himself and me (and while speaking to his daughter he had removed himself, magically, from being a mere subject in this drama of possessing). The Panama Canal has attached to it also the shameful qualities of imperialism and unjustified aggression, but all this, claim and counterclaim, was of no importance to my father, the idea and reality; "Panama Canal" he understood, it rolled off his tongue as if he had a rightful and just claim to it.

What does any of this have to do with the botanical garden or greenhouse? Often, when I am walking through a botanical garden, I come across a specimen or a replica of a landscape that makes me say to myself, Oh, this is the back yard of someone else, someone far away, someone's landscape the botanical garden can make an object. There

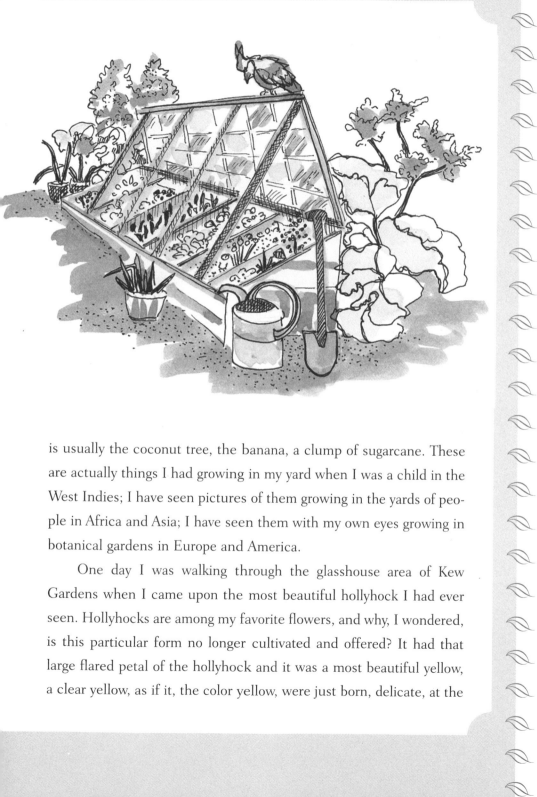

is usually the coconut tree, the banana, a clump of sugarcane. These are actually things I had growing in my yard when I was a child in the West Indies; I have seen pictures of them growing in the yards of people in Africa and Asia; I have seen them with my own eyes growing in botanical gardens in Europe and America.

One day I was walking through the glasshouse area of Kew Gardens when I came upon the most beautiful hollyhock I had ever seen. Hollyhocks are among my favorite flowers, and why, I wondered, is this particular form no longer cultivated and offered? It had that large flared petal of the hollyhock and it was a most beautiful yellow, a clear yellow, as if it, the color yellow, were just born, delicate, at the very beginning of its history as "yellow," but when I looked at the label on which its identification was written my whole being was sent a-whir. It was not a hollyhock at all but *Gossypium,* and its common name is cotton. Cotton all by itself exists in perfection, with malice toward none; in the sharp, swift, even brutal dismissive words of the botanist Oakes Ames, it is reduced to an economic annual, but the tormented, malevolent role it has played in my ancestral history is not forgotten by me. Even so, long after its role in the bondage of some of my ancestors had been eliminated, it continued to play a part in my life.

My mother had a friend who lived a long walk away from us, in what was considered "the country"; in Antiguan terms then, it meant a place where you could not see too many people from your own house. My mother's friend raised guinea hens, some pigs, and chickens. These animals were all unfriendly, sullen, not like animals in a picture book at all. In a large field beyond the house, beyond the yard where the animals lived, this woman grew a crop of cotton. I had never seen this cotton in bloom, I never even knew it had a flower. I saw the cotton only at harvest time, which coincided with my long school holidays sometime in July and August, and sometimes I was asked to reap it and, when it was all gathered up in large containers, to separate the cotton from its pod and then from its seed. There were many reasons why I came to hate this period of my young life: I was away from my mother and my family in general, I could see the graveyard from the house in which I was staying, the guinea hens were unfamiliar, the pigs were cross, the hens were unhappy, but perhaps the most lasting memory is the cotton. It had to be picked, and though I can't remember having to actually do that, pick the cotton, I can so well remember large clumps of it filling up a room, some of the clumps free of the dry pod and seed, some of the clumps waiting to be free of the dry pod and seed. I remember my hands aching, particularly in the area at the base of my thumbs, as I tried to separate dried pod from cotton, and then the almost certainly white cotton from its certainly black seed. They were inextricably bound, seed and fruit, and they were hard to separate. This is not a fiction; this all occurred to me while seeing this particular flower in bloom in Kew Gardens. I had never seen the cotton plant in bloom before. The hollyhock, to which it is related—they are in the same family, *Malvaceae*—is among my favorite perennials; perhaps the fact that the hollyhock looks like cotton when it is in flower is an explanation; on the other hand, the hollyhock could have been my least favorite perennial for the very same reason. I wait for the unknown expanse called time to let me know.

Accounts of botanical gardens begin with men who have sworn to forsake the company of women and have attached themselves to other things, the pursuit of only thinking, contemplating the world as it is or ought to be and, as a relief from this or complementary to this, the capture, isolation, and imprisoning of plants. This is my interpretation, this is the view I favor.

It was in a glasshouse, the glasshouse of a rich man named George Clifford, that Carolus Linnaeus, Adam like, invented modern plant nomenclature. He gave names to the things he saw growing before him. George Clifford lived in the Netherlands, and for reasons never made clear, he is always described as an Anglo-Dutch banker. The plants in his glasshouse could have come to him only through, and I quote from *The Oxford Companion to Gardens,* "the influence of the world trade being developed by maritime powers such as The

Netherlands and Great Britain." Exactly where the plants originated and what their names were before Linnaeus named them and the names he gave them, I do not know. I know they were not native to the Netherlands or Great Britain; if they had been, he would not have needed the glasshouse. The name Linnaeus is interesting; his family seems to have adopted it out of a special feeling an ancestor of his had toward the linden tree. Perhaps, then, the naming of plants was for him a matter of spiritual destiny.

I do not mind the glasshouse; I do not mind the botanical garden. This is not so grand a gesture on my part, it is mostly an admission of defeat: to mind would be completely futile, I cannot do anything about it anyway. I only mind the absence of this admission, this contradiction: perhaps every good thing that stands before us comes at a great cost to someone else.

IN HISTORY

What to call the thing that happened to me and all who look like me?

Should I call it history?

If so, what should history mean to someone like me?

Should it be an idea, should it be an open wound with each breath I take in and expel healing and opening the wound again and again, over and over, and is this healing and opening a moment that began in 1492 and has yet to come to an end? Is it a collection of facts, all true and precise details, and if so, when I come across these true and precise details, what should I do, how should I feel, where should I place myself?

Why should I be obsessed with all these questions?

My history begins like this: In 1492, Christopher Columbus discovered the New World.

Since this is only the beginning and I am not yet in the picture, I have not yet made an appearance, the word "discover" does not set off an alarm, I am not yet confused by this assertion. Discover is a fact that I accept; I am only taken by the personality of this quarrelsome, restless man. Who is he? His origins are sometimes obscure, sometimes no one knows just where he really came from, who he really was. His origins are sometimes quite vivid: his father was a tailor, he came from Genoa; as a boy, he wandered up and down the Genoese wharves, fascinated by sailors and their tales of faraway lands; these lands would be filled with treasures, all things far away are treasures. I am far away but I am not yet a treasure, I am not a part of this man's consciousness, he does not know of me, I do not yet have a name. And so the word "discover," as it is applied to this new world, remains uninteresting to me.

He, Christopher Columbus, then discovers this new world. That it is new only to him, that it had a substantial existence, physical and spiritual, before he became aware of it, does not occur to him. To cast blame on him now for this is childish, immature, small-minded, even with all the moral substance of a certificate given to a schoolgirl for good behavior; to be a well-behaved schoolgirl is not hard. When he sees this new world, it is really new to him; he has never seen anything like it before, it was not what he had expected, in his mind he had images of China and Japan, and though he thought he was in China and Japan, it was not the China or Japan he had fixed in his mind; he, after all, had never been to China and Japan ever. When he saw this new world, he couldn't find enough words to describe what was before him: the people were new, the flora and fauna were new, the way the water met the sky was new, this world itself was new. It was the New

World—but New only because he had never seen it before, new to him in a way even heaven itself could not have been.

"If one does not know the names, one's knowledge of things is useless." This is attributed to Isidorus, and I do not know if this is the Greek Isidorus or the other Isidorus, the Archbishop of Seville; but why not put it another way: To have knowledge of things, one must first give them a name. This, in any case, seems to me to have been Christopher Columbus's principle, for he named and he named; he named places, he named people, he named things. This world he saw before him had a blankness to it, the blankness of the newly made, the newly born. It had no before. I could say it had no history, but I would have to begin again, I would have to ask the question again: What is history? This blankness, the one Columbus met, was more like the blankness of paradise; paradise emerges from chaos and chaos is not history, chaos is the opposite of the legitimate order of things. Paradise, then, is an arrangement of the ordinary and the extraordinary, but in such a way as to make it, paradise, seem as if it had fallen out of the clear air. Nothing about it suggests the messy life of the builder, the carpenter, the quarrels with the contractor, the people who are late with the delivery of materials, the whole project going over budget, the small disappointments to be found in details of the end result. This is an unpleasant arrangement, this is not paradise. Paradise is the thing just met when all the troublesome details have been vanquished, over-come; paradise is the place that does not hold any of the difficulties you have known before; it holds nothing, only happiness, and it never reveals that even happiness is a burden, eventually.

Christopher Columbus met paradise. It would not have been par-adise for the people living there; they would have had the ordinary dreariness of living anywhere day after day, the ordinary dreariness of just being alive. But someone else's ordinary dreariness is another person's epiphany.

The way in which he wanted to know these things was not in the way of satisfying curiosity or correcting ignorance; he wanted to know them to possess them, and he wanted to possess them in a way that must have been a surprise to him. His ideas kept not so much changing as evolving; he wanted to prove the world was round, even to know with certainty that the world was round, that it did not come to an abrupt end at a sharp cliff from which one could fall into nothing. And then after the world was proved round, this round world should belong to his patrons, the King and Queen of Spain. And then, finding himself at the other side of the globe and far away from his patrons, he loses himself, for it becomes clear that the person who really can name the thing gives it a life, a reality, that it did not have before. His patrons are in Spain, looking at the balance sheet: if they invest so much, will his journey yield a return to make the investment worthwhile? But he—I am still speaking of Columbus—is in the presence of something else.

His task is easier than he thought it would be, his task is harder than he could have imagined. If only he had really reached Japan or China—for to him places like that already had an established narrative. It was not a narrative these places had established themselves; it was a narrative someone like him had invented, Marco Polo, for instance. But this world, China or Japan, in the same area of the world to him, had an order and the order offered comfort, the recognizable is always so comforting. But this new place, what was it? Sometimes he thought it was just like Seville, Spain; sometimes it was like Seville, only more so; sometimes it was more beautiful than Seville. Mostly it was "marvelous," and this word "marvelous" is the word he uses again and again, and when he uses it, what the reader (and that is what I have been, a reader of this account of a journey, and the account is by Columbus himself) can feel, can hear, can see, is a great person whose small soul has been sundered by something unexpected. And yet the unexpected turns out to be the most ordinary thing: people, the sky, the sun, the land, the water surrounding the land, the things growing on the land.

What were the things growing on the land? I pause for this. What were the things growing on that land and why do I pause for this?

I come from a place called Antigua. I shall speak of it as if I had never heard of it before, I shall speak of it as if no one has ever heard of it before, I shall speak of it as if it is just new. In the writings, in anything representing a record of the imagination of Christopher Columbus, I cannot find any expectation of a place like this. It is a small lump of insignificance, green, green, green, and green again. Let me describe this landscape again: it is green, and unmistakably so; another person who had a more specific interest, a painter, might say, It is a green that often verges on blue, it is a green that is often modified by reds and yellows and even other more intense or other shades of green. To me, it is green and green and green again. I have no interest other than this immediate and urgent one: the landscape is green. For it is on this green landscape that suddenly I and the people who look like me make an appearance.

I, me, the person writing now, started to think of all this while really focused on something and someone else altogether. I was standing in my garden; my garden is in a place called Vermont; it is in a village situated in a place called Vermont. From the point of view of growing things—that is, from the gardener's point of view—Vermont is vastly different from that other place I am native to, Antigua. But while standing in that place, Vermont, I think about the place I am from, Antigua. Christopher Columbus never saw Vermont at all, it never entered his imagination. He saw Antigua, I believe on a week-day, but if not, then it would have been on a Sunday, for in this life there would have been only weekdays or Sundays, but he never set foot on it, he only came across it while passing by. My world, then, the only world I might have known if circumstances had not intervened, entered human imagination—the human imagination that I am famil-iar with, the one that dominates the world in which I live—as a foot-note to someone just passing by. By the time Christopher Columbus got to the place where I am from, the place which forms the founda-tion of the person writing this, he was exhausted, he was sick of the whole thing, he longed for his old home, or longed just to sit still and enjoy the first few things he had come upon; the first few things he had come upon were a lot. The first few things he had come upon were named after things prominent in his thinking, his sponsors espe-cially; when he came to the place I am from, he had been reduced to memorializing a place of worship; the place I am from is named after a church. This church might have been an important church to Christopher Columbus, but churches were not important, originally, to people who look like me. And if people who look like me have an inheritance, part of this inheritance involves this confusion of intent: we were on his mind when he set out from his point of embarkation (for him, too, there is no origin, he originates from Italy, he sails from Spain, and this is the beginning of another now-traditional American narrative, point of origin and point of embarkation): "Here is something I have never seen before, I especially like it because it has no precedent, but it is frightening because it has no precedent, and so to make it less frightening I will frame it in terms of the thing I know; I know a church, I know the name of the church; even if I do not like or know the people connected to this, the church, it is more familiar to me, this church, than the very ground I am standing on; the ground has changed, but the church, which is in my mind, remains the same."

I, the person writing this now, close the quotation marks. Up to this point I (and those who look like me) am not yet a part of this narrative. I can observe these events—a man sets sail with three ships, and after many, many days on the ocean finds new lands whose existence he had never even heard of before, and then, finding in these new lands people and their things, people and things he had never heard of before, he empties the land of these people. It is when the land is completely empty that I and the people who look like me begin to make an appearance, the food I eat begins to make an appearance, the trees I will see each day come from far away and begin to make an appearance; the sky is as it always was, the sun is as it always was, the water surrounding the land on which I am just making an appearance is as it always was, but these are the only things that are left from before that man sailing with his three ships reached the land on which I eventually make my appearance.

When did I begin to ask all this? When did I begin to think of all this and in just this way? What is history? Is it a theory? I no longer live in the place where I and those that look like me first made an appearance. I live in another place. It has another narrative. Its narrative, too, can start with that man sailing on his ships for days and days, for that man sailing on his ships for days and days is the source of many narratives, he was like a deity in the simplicity of his beliefs, in the simplicity of his actions; just listen to the straightforward way many volumes featuring this man sailing on his ships begin: "In fourteen hundred and ninety-two . . . In fourteen hundred and ninety-two." But it was while standing in this other place that has a narrative mostly different from the narrative of the place in which I make an appearance that I began to think of this.

One day, while looking at the things that lay at my feet, I was having an argument with myself over the names I should use when referring to the things that lay before me. These things were plants. The plants, all of them—and there were hundreds—had two names: they had a common name, that is, a name assigned to them by people for whom these plants have value, and then they had a proper name, or a Latin name, a name assigned to them by an agreed-on group of botanists. For a long time I resisted using the proper names of the things that lay before me. I believed that it was an affectation to say *Eupatorium* when you could say joe-pye weed, and I would only say joe-pye weed. The botanists are from the same part of the world as the man who sailed on the three ships, the man who started the narrative from which I trace my beginning. And in a way, too, the botanists are like that man who sailed on the ships: they emptied worlds of their names; they emptied the worlds of things animal, vegetable, and mineral of their names and replaced these names with names pleasing to them; these names are pleasing to them because they are reasonable; reason is a pleasure to them.

Carolus Linnaeus was born on the twenty-third of May 1707, somewhere in Sweden. (I know where, but I like the high-handedness of not saying so.) His father's name was Nils Ingemarson, his family were farmers. Apparently in Sweden then, surnames were uncommon among ordinary people, and so a farmer would add "son" to his name, or he was called after the farm on which he lived. Nils Ingemarson became a Lutheran minister, and on doing so he wanted to have a proper surname, not just a name with "son" attached to it. On his family farm grew a linden tree. It had grown there for generations and had come to be regarded with reverence among neighboring farmers; people believed that misfortune would fall on you if you harmed this tree in any way. This linden tree was so well regarded that people passing by used to pick twigs that had dropped from it and carefully place them at the base of the tree. Nils Ingemarson took his surname from this tree, Linnaeus is the Latinized form of the Swedish word *lind*. Other branches of this family who also needed a surname drew inspiration from this tree; some took the name Tiliander, the Latin word for linden is *tilia;* and then some others who also needed a surname took the name Lindelius from the Swedish word *lind,* which means linden.

Carolus Linnaeus's father had a garden; I do not know what his mother had. His father loved growing things in this garden and would point them out to the young Carolus, but when the young Carolus could not remember the names of the plants, his father gave him a scolding and told him he would not tell him the names of any more plants. (Is this story true? How could it not be?) He grew up not far from a forest filled with beech, a forest with pine, a grove filled with oaks, meadows. His father had a collection of rare plants in his garden (but what would be rare to him and in that place I do not know). At the time Linnaeus was born, Sweden, this small country that I now think of as filled with well-meaning and benign people, interested mainly in the well-being of children and the well-being of the unfortunate, no matter their age, was the ruler of an empire; but the remains of it are visible now only in the architecture of the main squares of the capitals of places like Estonia. And so what to make of all this, the small detail that is the linden tree, the large expanse of the Swedish empire, and a small boy whose father was a Lutheran pastor? At the beginning of this narrative, the narrative that is Linnaeus, I have not yet made an appearance, the Swedes are not overly implicated in the Atlantic slave trade, not because they did not want to be but only because they weren't allowed to be, other people were better at it than they.

He was called "the little botanist" because he would neglect his studies and go out looking at flowers; if even then he had already showed an interest in naming and classifying plants, or the ability to do so, this fact is not in any account of his life that I have come across. He went to university at Uppsala, he studied there with Olof Rudbeck. I can pause at this name, Rudbeck, and say rudbeckia, and say, I do not like rudbeckia, I never have it in my garden, but then I remember that a particularly stately, beautiful yellow flower, *Rudbeckia nitida,* grows in a corner of my field garden. Linnaeus met Anders Celsius (the Celsius scale of temperature measurement), who was so taken with Linnaeus's knowledge of botany that he gave Linnaeus free lodging in his house. Linnaeus became one of the youngest lecturers at his university. He went to Lapland and collected plants and insects native to that region of the world; he wrote and published an account of it called *Flora Lapponica.* In Lapland he acquired a set of clothing that people native to that region of the world wore on festive occasions; I have seen a picture of him dressed in these clothes, the caption under the picture says that he is wearing his Lapland costume. Suddenly I am made a little uneasy, for just when is it that other people's clothes become your costume. But I am not too uneasy, I haven't really entered this narrative yet, though I shall soon; in any case, I do not know the Laplanders, they live too far away, they do not look like me.

I enter the picture only when Linnaeus takes a boat to Holland. He becomes the doctor of an obviously neurotic man (obvious only to me, I arbitrarily deem him so; no account of him I have ever come across has described him so) named George Clifford. George Clifford is often described as a rich merchant banker—just like that, a rich merchant banker—and this description often seems to say that a rich merchant banker is merely a type of person one could be, an ordinary type of person, anyone could be that. And now how to go on, for on hearing that George Clifford was a rich merchant in the eighteenth century, I am sure I have become a part of the narrative of the binomial system of plant nomenclature.

George Clifford had glasshouses full of vegetable materials from all over the world. This is what Linnaeus wrote of them:

> I was greatly amazed when I entered the greenhouses, full as they were of so many plants that a son of the North must feel bewitched, and wonder to what strange quarter of the globe he had been transported. In the first house were cultivated an abundance of flowers from southern Europe, plants from Spain, the South of France, Italy, Sicily and the isles of Greece. In the second were treasures from Asia,

such as Poincianas, cocoanut and other palms, etc; in the third, Africa's strangely shaped, not to say misshapen plants, such as the numerous forms of Aloe and Mesembryanthemum families, carnivorous flowers, Euphorbias, Crassula and Proteas species, and so on. And finally in the fourth greenhouse were grown the charming inhabitants of America and the rest of the New World; large masses of Cactus varieties, orchids, cruciferea, yams, magnolias, tulip-trees, calabash trees, cassias, acacias, tamarinds, pepper-plants, Anona, manicinilla, cucurbitaceous trees and many other, and surrounded by these, plantains, the most stately of all the world's plants, the most beauteous Hernandia, silver gleaming species of Protea and camphor trees. When I then entered the positively royal residence and the extremely instructive museum, whose collections no less spoke in their owner's praise, I, a stranger, felt completely enraptured, as I had never before seen its like. My heart-felt wish was that I might lend a helping hand with its management.

In almost every account of an event that has taken place sometime in the last five hundred years there is always a moment when I feel like placing an asterisk somewhere in its text and at the end of the official story making my own addition. This chapter in the history of botany is such a moment. But where shall I begin? George Clifford is interesting—shall I look at him? He long ago entered my narrative, I now feel I must enter his. What could it possibly mean to be a merchant banker in the eighteenth century? He is sometimes described as making his fortune in spices. Only once have I come across an account of him that says he was a director of the Dutch East India Company. The Dutch East India Company would not have been involved in the Atlantic trade in human cargo from Africa, but human cargo from Africa was a part of world trade. To read a brief account of the Dutch East India trading company in my very old encyclopedia is not unlike reading the label on an old can of paint. The entry mentions dates, the names of Dutch governors or people acting in the Dutch interest; it mentions trade routes, places, commodities, incidents of war between the Dutch and other European people, it never mentions the people who lived in the area of the Dutch trading factories, places like Ceylon, Java, the Cape of Good Hope are emptied of their people as the landscape itself was emptied of the things they were familiar with, the things that Linnaeus found in George Clifford's greenhouse.

"If one does not know the names, one's knowledge of things is useless." It was in George Clifford's greenhouse that Linnaeus gave some things names. The Adam-like quality of this effort was not lost on him. "We revere the Creator's omnipotence," he says, meaning, I think, that he understood he had not made the things he was describing, he was only giving them names. And even as a relationship exists between George Clifford's activity in the world, the world as it starts out on ships leaving the seaports of the Netherlands, traversing the earth's seas, touching on the world's peoples and the places they are in, the things that have meant something to them being renamed, and a whole new set of narratives imposed on them, narratives that place them at a disadvantage in relationship to George Clifford and his fellow Dutch—even as I can say all this in one breath or in one large volume, does not an invisible thread, a thread that no deep breath or large volume can contain, reach between Carolus Linnaeus, his father's desire to give himself a distinguished name, the name then coming from a tree, the linden tree, a tree whose existence was regarded as out of the ordinary, and his invention of a system of naming that even I am forced to use?

The invention of this system has been a good thing. Its narrative would begin in this way: In the beginning, the vegetable kingdom was chaos, people everywhere called the same things by a name that made sense to them, not by a name arrived at by an objective standard. But who has an interest in an objective standard? Who needs one? It makes me ask again, What to call the thing that happened to me and all who look like me? Should I call it history? And if so, what should history mean to someone who looks like me? Should it be an idea; should it be an open wound, each breath I take in and expel healing and opening the wound again, over and over, or is it a long moment that begins anew each day since 1492?

PART III

A LETTER TO DAN HINKLEY AND ROBERT JONES, THE PROPRIETORS OF HERONSWOOD NURSERY

6 March 1996

Dear Dan and Robert,

I am back at home from my million-mile tour. If there was any justice to these things, I would get so rich that I would never have to do it again. But there is no justice and there never will be, so there. It was wonderful to see you both, though, and then to see Dan in California. My purchases from Western Hills Nursery in Occidental, California, returned with me all safe and sound. I felt very sorry for them being locked up in a box as I made my way from one luxurious hotel to the next, but I just pretended they were in the post office. I heard about Dan's purchases at the Stryben Arboretum the next day; they were that noticeable. I am only sad that I wasn't there to witness it. To see a top desirer (is there such a word?) of flora in action is quite fun, I think.

To speak of desire: is there anything I should have that I do not know about and you are about to sell the last of? Please add it to my list. I trust you both completely. What about that rose with the scarlet canes? *Ooowww.* Two things, requests. Dan, I am going to Holland in

the middle of April, would you still like to send me to those nurserymen to see their plants and their gardens? If you are too busy to bother with it just now, pay it no mind; I will be happy anyway seeing masses of tulips. I love tulips. And what

is the best time to see a garden in England, just before the end of June or just after the end of June? I am bearing in mind the symposium, and the chance to see Dan (though I will be sad not to see Robert) and feed him Edna Lewis's corn pudding.

Is it March where you both are? It is March here and winter is behaving like me when I am somewhere I like to be and can sense that I am making all my companions miserable by not behaving and not knowing it is time to leave. I shall go now.

Love to you both, Jamaica

SPRING

It was a day in early spring, the first really spring-like day since spring arrived, and my children and I were sitting in the sun watching two seemingly very young rabbits (they were small) cavort on the grass, which was half brown, half green. They, the two rabbits, chased each other, nipping at tails, biting necks, leaping in the air together and colliding, and my children were so delighted and amazed with this sight; I sat with them with a grin on my face that was really a grimace. In fact, I was thinking, especially when I saw one rabbit chasing the other into the area that is my vegetable garden: How I wish that I could transform myself into an enormous, vividly striped animal that with a few bounds could approach the cavorting rabbits and, with a playful swat of my large paw, grab them and playfully toss them into the air. The joy I would get from hearing the snap-snap of their little necks breaking in midair would be immeasurable. When I told Annie, my daughter, this, she said, "Jeez, Mom, that is really mean." But how mean is it really (I did not say this to her), after all I found small collections of their droppings in all the flower beds, and I am convinced that only the delightful stink of the fritillarias (the smell of the underarms of ten people you love) that I planted here, there, and everywhere, kept them away from things they would have liked to eat.

The winter was unbearable, as usual, but this one just past seemed an exaggeration. The sky was always too low, too gray, the ground was always too high (it was the snow) and too white. The days were too short and dark, the nights were too long and darker still. Then one day, by the calendar, it was spring; not too long after that, an actual spring-like day appeared. The sun felt as if it really did give off heat, the first time in almost half a year I could say that with certainty. The grass seemed to turn green before my eyes. The last mound of snow near the edge of the field melted away fast. But winter, like a tiresome person who isn't much liked in the first place, would not quite go away. The air still had a chill in it that I no longer had the strength to steel myself against, and so I felt more cold than I did in January. And then all at once the magic of daylight saving time did something wonderful: the day became longer and brighter even as it ended; as the remains of winter clung to the top of the hills, the line of blue and purple mist created by the trees crept up higher and higher. One day I saw an orange spot moving about the yard and I ran to the window and shouted, "The robins are here," and the other members of my family, who were in the room also, looked at me, and though they would never speak ill of me to each other, I could see they were silently wondering if I was crazy.

And on that day when it was really spring, it was all about us, everything that was still alive was in bud, and the sun was warm, we were sitting in it and had to take off our jackets, it was possible to see some of what had survived the winter. All my roses were alive. I was especially pleased to see the roses 'Ballerina' and 'Cécile Brünner,' which many people had told me I could not grow in this climate, covered with the small red pimples of new growth. I have really learned this as a gardener: listen to everyone and then grow the things you love. I have learned as much through my own conceitedness and from my own mistakes as I have from all the great gardeners I have met. I have learned that though I live in zone 5, parts of my garden have a microclimate of their own that places them in zone 6.

One day the air was glistening, shimmering, with tints of red, green, yellow, blue from the budding trees. The sun had climbed up, making its long way across the sky. It was warm, it was May. Snakes in pairs emerged from the stone wall and from in between the stone steps, and sat all coiled up in that perfect way so typical of them, inspiring fear and admiration. I am afraid of snakes and so have the impulse to kill them all immediately, but then I remember their predatory nature; I saw one of them slithering across the lawn to the place where I believe a family of shrews live (I am even more afraid of rodents than I am of snakes). The month of May comes on suddenly and moves along swiftly, and each day pleasure after pleasure is flung before my eyes with such intensity that after the barrenness and harshness, in varying degrees, of the months before, it seems mocking, a punishment, to look out and see the bergenia, pink and white against the bleeding heart, pink and white; the stiff pink flower of the umbrella plant (*Peltiphyllum peltatum,* a plant introduced to me by Joe

Eck and Wayne Winterrowd), followed by large leaves held up by long, elegant stems; the pink and blue, white and mauve of the pulmonarias ('Mrs. Moon,' 'Janet Fisk,' 'Sissinghurst White'); the emerging green tips of the hosta, missile-like in shape, slow in progress as the snails who so like to nibble at their tender shoots; the flowering apple trees. The forget-me-nots had happily spread in a part of the garden among the queen of the prairie (*Filipendula rubra* 'Venusta') and lupine and plume poppy (*Macleaya*), and their little blue heads among the varying shades of green were so strikingly beautiful, so simple, the pleasure in them so immediate, that it took me many minutes to mistrust it; how long would it be before some other thought would come along and undermine my delight?

And then again, one day, another warm day, as I was standing in the children's sandbox, which is under an extremely tall hemlock, I suddenly heard the angry screech of a bird; I recognized the sound of

a mother feeling the beings she loves are in danger, and so I looked up and found the nest just above my head. I could not see what was in it, chicks or eggs, but I felt much sympathy and tried to tell her that even though I did not like her eating the sweet peas when I had just planted them and hunting down my earthworms, she was in no danger from me, she and all who looked like her were quite safe with me. That is May, the month I love the most, and when my turn comes to make the world, as surely it will, I shall make my May ninety days long. December, January, and February shall be allotted ten hours each; I have not finalized my plans for the other months, but none of them shall exceed May.

A visit to Carlson's Gardens (a nursery in South Salem, New York, specializing in azaleas, rhododendrons and kalmias) yielded not the stern, forbidding, opinionated Mr. Carlson I knew from the telephone but a gentle, warm man who indulged me in all my erroneous opinions about the hardiness of some plants I had been considering planting, before humorously correcting and guiding me in a most fatherly way, really, toward what would serve me best. When every once in a while I would say something that he knew to be correct, he would look at me and nod and smile and say simply, "That's right, that's right," and I would just beam inside with pride, reminding myself of the small, eager, anxious child I used to be. The rhododendrons 'Janet Blair,' 'Caroline Gable,' and 'Scintillation' were opening up. Those would be well suited to my hardiness zone, Mr. Carlson said. In his garden they towered over me, spreading themselves out wantonly; he had planted his twenty-five years ago. The plants I could buy to bring home in the trunk of a car were not even as big as my children. If only I could know now what I will be in love with in twenty-five years; in that way I could arrange everything now so that I could have maximum enjoyment then. I bought three *R. schlippenbachii*.

Long before all that, I had overwhelmed Jack Manix at Walker Farms with all the seeds I had ordered from various seed houses and sent to him to grow for me. He lives on the farm that his family has owned and worked for many generations. Much of his land is now not farmed at all, and the state of Vermont has cast a jealous eye on it, judging it just the right place to put a dump. It is the fault of all the other people who have moved to Vermont with their families, people like me, who wouldn't harm anyone directly. Jack Manix never complained to me about his embattled condition, he only marveled at the amount of seeds I had sent him. I had ordered fifteen different kinds of foxgloves from Thompson & Morgan, five different kinds of primroses, daturas, meconopsis (Jack said he wasn't sure he could make this germinate at all), seeds of poppies from Pine Tree Gardens in Maine, and the only place where I also found seeds for *Artemisia annua* (Sweet Annie). I had ordered about five different kinds of daturas, meaning to share them with a friend, but after she read a hysterical account by Allen Lacy (in *Home Ground*) of the dangers this plant poses to children and the danger it had posed to early settlers of America, she refused to take any of them. (Even though I pointed out to her that where I come from the datura is an obnoxious weed inhabiting and colonizing every vacant spot of ground where nothing else will grow and that I have never heard of children or anyone else dying from it, but I have heard of children and others dying of malnutrition, she would not change her mind.)

There was rain and it came down in that unwelcome way of something necessary but just not needed at that moment, which led to complaints and all other kinds of fretting, because perhaps some things would rot and other things not germinate at all. None of those fears were realized, but there were an overwhelming number of blue-and-gray fat-bodied bugs sucking nectar from the buds of the lupines and the rosebuds, and one morning before the sun came up, after the children had boarded a bus to school, I killed them all by myself with doses of insecticidal soap. On one of those rainy days when I could not work outside, I had peered into a dark corner of the garden, made even darker by the weather itself, and I thought of blue-leaf hostas, and so called up Mr. Ruh at Sunnybrook Farms in Wisconsin, a nursery specializing in hostas. In particular, he and Mrs. Ruh list in their catalogue this: "The Tardiana of Eric Smith" and with the simple question of What is the Tardiana of Eric Smith? I stepped into a sort of family controversy. Mr. Ruh told me that Eric Smith was a gardener and hosta hybridizer who eventually bred some of the bluest of the blue-leaf hostas. He, Eric Smith, was the gardener (that is, the working hand) to a famous gardener (that is, the person who owned the garden), but instead of doing his work (gardening) he kept breeding hostas. The person for whom he worked hated hostas, and was fed up with his neglectfulness, in any case, and so fired him; Smith in a fit (of anger perhaps) threw all his experiments into the compost and went home. Shortly after that, he died, and some time after that, his experiments were found in the compost. But he left no notes on what he had done, and so only through speculating and guessing has it been possible to duplicate his work. Mr. Ruh was not at all sad to tell me the name of the gardener who fired Eric Smith. Money—i.e., not having enough of it—prevented me from ordering Eric Smith's hostas; they cost at least fifteen dollars per plant. I have never seen his hostas, but I understand Eric Smith's story of the fanatic, misunderstood lover against the ignorant world. In the book *The Genus Hosta* by W. George Schmid, under Eric Smith's entry I read this: "H. Tardiana grex Smith UK: This group of hybrids was initially given the name the hybrid binomial H. x tardiana, but this name is illegitimate for several reasons . . ."; it then goes off into a gentlemanly distancing of Eric Smith from the world of real hostas. That day, a combination of moist, cold, and warm brought out the slugs, and I collected them with my own impassioned sense of grievance against them (they had eaten the delphiniums, the ligularia) in a jar; that night the children and I laid them out on the slabs of marble that make up a walk just outside my back door and sprinkled teaspoons of salt on them; they wriggled and squirmed before turning into a brown liquid. I encouraged the children's squeals and laughter, but what I really heard were the silent screams of the slugs as they struggled into oblivion. Even as I wish never to see another slug in my garden again, I look forward to another day.

Families are a malevolent lot, no matter the permutations they make, no matter the shape they take, no matter how beautiful they look, no matter the nice things they say.

WHERE TO BEGIN?

Where to begin? The rhododendron 'Jane Grant' arrived; on a Tuesday, while on the way to Rocky Dale Farm, a very special nursery here in Vermont, I learned that it is always closed on that particular day—Tuesday; I had ordered three dicentra 'Snowdrift' from two different places and they were meant for the same place, but I did not realize this until the day they arrived, which was on the same day at the same time. What to do?

The rhododendron 'Jane Grant' is among the most beautiful of plants I have ever received in the mail, and that is hardly the way to judge a plant on first sight, even though that way works very well with people, but immediately, as I unwrapped her from her brown wrapping, I almost wept. She was beautiful, all delicate and tidy; glossy, medium-green leaves with a lush indumentum (*R. yakushimanum* is a parent), and perched on top of the leaves, a generous fist of blossoms, whitish, limy green now, eventually opening, becoming a succession of pinks (as I write this, the transformation has not yet begun), all of them reminding me of something pleasurable: a girl's dress, the inside of a mouth, a moment very, very early in the morning when light from the sun itself is in doubt. I had resisted this shrub for so long. And why? Jane Grant, the woman it is named for, used to be married to the first editor of *The New Yorker*. At this very moment I can't remember why I resisted a plant only because it is named after the wife of the first editor of *The New Yorker*. And this only underlines for me the flabby basis on which so many of my opinions and decisions rest, so flabby I don't even remember them. I ordered the 'Jane Grant' one day in January when I was recovering from pneumonia and trying to cheer myself up by looking at pictures of flowers for sale, not pictures of flowers already growing in someone else's garden. I saw it beautifully pictured in the White Flower Farm catalogue and ordered it (along with many other things, none of them breaking any other prohibitions, as far as I could tell), and on the day that I returned from a nursery in Quiche, Vermont (a compensation for the Rocky Dale nursery disappointment), I met my 'Jane Grant' and many other huge boxes filled with plants from all the nurseries I had ordered from on that day in January. There is no doubt that everyone can have an interesting garden simply by ordering through the Wayside and White Flower Farm catalogues, but to have a garden made up of unusual native (American) plants and plants from other parts of the world, particularly Japan, Korea, and China, you have to go to some smaller, less-well-known nurseries, such as Heronswood (in Washington),

Arrowhead Alpines (in Michigan), Plants Delight Nursery (in North Carolina). If you find ephedra worth growing, you will not be able to purchase one from Wayside or White Flower. The Plants Delight Nursery lists four different kinds. I bought mine from Arrowhead Alpines.

On that Tuesday when all the plants I had ordered from seeing their pictures arrived, I was not at home to receive them and immediately remove them from their cardboard prison, and provide for them a refreshment of water and a sheltered place. No. I was on my way to Rocky Dale Farm, a legendary nursery among gardeners here in Vermont. It is far away from where I live, and so I was going with a friend, who not only is unafraid to drive herself long distances (I am) but has a truck. On our way there, she had the good sense to call and see if Rocky Dale was open; they were not. Then she had the good sense to think of our going instead to Talbot's, another nursery, just outside Quiche, Vermont. Talbot's is a well-kept secret. Mr. Talbot is a botanist, and in the winter he gives lectures on growing plants. I had never met the Talbots before, and on the spot I made up my mind that they were so appealing—if only I lived next door. After spending many hours choosing the plants I wanted to buy (flowering quince 'Cameo,' a fern-leaf lilac, two fern-leaf peonies, some *Petasites gigantea,* some ornamental rhubarb, two kinds of yellow monkshood, three different grasses, some woodland phlox, some tiarella, a katsura tree, some pussy willow with black catkins, among other things), I decided that they, the Talbots, were not unlike characters I meet in a good book and find appealing, comfortable, cozy, no matter what their faults, all their faults of course falling within reason, which is to say, not unlike my own. On our way home, my friend was annoyed at me. I had bought too many things, she thought. She didn't say so. I could see it on her face. But only in very rare circumstances must plants be bought in ones. The minimum is three, preferably five, and then up from that. To me, in a garden almost everything by itself is wrong. If it is very beautiful, more of it will do. If space limits it to one, then you must just say so. The feeling against planting only one must be widespread. When you must plant only one of anything, you are told to regard it as a specimen; but a specimen is so unfamiliar, so unwarm, so ungardenlike. One of anything, children, plants, is so tight-fisted I could cry.

One day Mr. Harrington (Ken, not his brother Phil) came to my house and removed from various parts of the yard the rubbishy honeysuckle shrub, a large old pine tree that grew just outside the window of my son's room (this was not a wanton act on my part, an act dictated solely by my obsession with the landscape; the large branches of this tree would rub against the windowpane and frighten my son); an old lilac shrub was dug out from one place and put somewhere else; he remade the driveway. It took him many days to do all this, and as he made the many places bare, I plotted the many things I could put in them. Along the road where the honeysuckle used to be I had decided to put in a hedge of buckthorn, but then I turned against this when I saw what was said about buckthorn in that tyrannical volume *The Manual of Woody Landscape Plants* by Michael Dirr. Is there a gardener who knows about this book who can resist the opinions expressed in it? My friends and I can hardly plant a shrub or tree of any kind without saying to each other, "What does Dirr say?" In the case of my buckthorn, what Dirr had to say resulted in my canceling an order of twenty buckthorn plants from Roger and Penny at the

Equinox Valley Nursery. And even before I settled on the buckthorn, I had wanted to plant a hedge of arrowwood viburnum (*V. dilatatum*), but the Dirr is very scornful. Looking up from the Dirr, I was so comforted to see Mr. Harrington sitting in his bulldozer, driving his big truck or just whacking away at something, his wife and son taking his directions with great care. He is such a nice man. He loves trees, no matter what they are, as long as they have a good form, which the honeysuckle does not. He reminds me that there are two kinds of Vermonters: native Vermonters, people who look very much like each other but not in a disturbing way, not in a way that makes you feel so bad if you do not look like them; and then the rest of us, who have recently arrived in Vermont, and we all look like people in a witness protection program, that is to say, if we were seen while in Vermont, by people who know us not in Vermont, we would appear to be almost looking like ourselves. To live in Vermont without being born here means that one beautiful day in spring you were driving through, as I did on my way to the Talbots', and saw so many beautiful houses set in the middle of so many beautiful views that you bought one of them. And then waiting to be discovered is: JANUARY! FEBRUARY! MAAAAAAARCH!

On those days when Mr. Harrington was helping me rearrange the small patches of my land, I walked around with a pencil and paper and did something I always thought too pretentious to even consider: I made drawings of my garden, or rather, I connected a series of lines to each other, and inside the lines I wrote down the names of shrubs and herbaceous plants I wanted to plant. I have now passed the point of planting only things I love without any prior regard as to how they will all look together. But still, my garden lacks something: it needs more shape, it needs more interesting things in its more shape. I started with around the house and in the back of the house and alongside the house; now I wish to move away from the house, go away from the house down to the bog, but still be connected to the house, I must never really leave the house. So, too, as I started with clematis 'Nelly Moser,' I now want *Clematis marmoraria*. I have fallen in love with

species. They are harder to like, being always only themselves, and when taken out of their own context, untidy nature, and placed in the orderliness of a garden, where they are mostly meant to prop up the jellylike personality of the owner of the house, they in turn appear frail, not as floriferous as they should be, or much too vigorous, another way of saying a weed, another way of saying "annoying." But I now want that very species, or plants not too far removed from that very thing. All this leads me to Bob and Brigitta Stewart and their

Arrowhead Alpines nursery in Fowlerville, Michigan. It was while visiting them one day in late April that I purchased some *Peltoboykinia* (for me, this meant a step away from the rodgersia), some *Primula farinosa,* some corydalis, some *Campanula betulaefolia,* two mertensia, lots of *Primula auricula,* ephedra, a *Paeonia peregrina*, a *Paeonia lutea,* three *Gentiana lutea.* To walk around the Arrowhead Alpines nursery, with Bob and Brigitta, in and out of their greenhouses, is to go down the road of plants in a way from which you can never really return. He picks up something I have never heard of and mentions its connection to a man named Josef Halder, a Czech botanist who had excellent access to the parts of Asia that were formerly under Soviet rule. Josef Halder is the ephedra plant discoverer. Bob mentions Eric Smith and his work with hellebores. I happen to be devoted to Eric Smith, but only because of what I know about his work with hostas. Eric Smith hostas are mainly the blue ones, and I try to have as many of his hostas as I can afford. They are not cheap. Bob then told me of a nursery I must visit; the nursery is in Scotland and is run by a man named Jim Archibald, who knew Eric Smith. It was with Jim Archibald that Eric Smith worked on hellebores. While walking through his greenhouse with Bob, being introduced to a vast treasury of plants for the garden that until then were unknown to me (*Mutisia spinosa,* for instance; it may not be altogether hardy for me, but I know how to manage that), I met a man named Jim, and he was bent over a tray trying to see if finally some of the seeds he had received from a plant-hunting expedition in which he had bought shares were germinating. They were not.

March came to an end in mid-May. None of my fritillarias bloomed, but I loved the bluish-green of the leaves of the *Persicarias* and the water-diluted green of the leaves of *F. imperialis.* The *Primula veris,* planted last year in June and grown from seeds I gave to Jack Manix, bloomed in a patch at the edge of a very old hemlock. Some daffodils I had bought for $1.50 at Whitman's Feed Store (North Bennington, Vermont) bloomed. I had not paid much attention when buying them, for it was way past the time when any bulb should have been put in the ground and I only bought them as an after-thought, to fill in a spot (I was just beginning to understand the idea of underplanting). These daffodils turned out to be 'Mount Hood,' the most beautiful daffodil I have ever seen, or rather have ever liked. They start out yellow and then change—not fade, but change—to a spectacular ivory, the shade of dinnerware on a shelf, tempting a child to see just how it would look shattered into many pieces. I do not like daffodils for a reason that is not at all aesthetic, a reason much more serious than that. The rodgersia returned, stubby, crooked fin-gers piercing through the ground. The pulmonarias bloomed so spec-tacularly I was sure they belonged to someone else. *Pulmonaria* 'Janet Fisk' and 'Mrs. Moon' have seeded; shall I now wait to see if one of the seedlings is a sport of some sort? But I am not at all interested in such a thing.

However. On the day I returned from the Talbots', I met the plants I had ordered from the White Flower Farm and Wayside nurs-eries. Those orders, along with the many plants I had just bought from the Talbots, along with some other plants Jack Manix had grown for me, were lined up on the floor of the garage, spilling out onto quite a bit of the driveway. The plants were in small pots, large pots, trays of six packs. It was not a pretty sight. When you look at a garden this is not what comes to mind. The children complained, and underneath their worry was the milk-money problem: had their mother spent all the money on plants, would they be hungry? They see the garden as the thing that stands between them and true happiness: my absolute attention.

Looking at all these plants spilling out of the garage at my feet, I thought of some people I know of who are connected with plants, and this was not in comparison, for it doesn't bear it, I just thought of them: George Clifford, the possessor of an enormous greenhouse in Amsterdam who had employed Linnaeus, thus giving him the opportunity to invent the binomial system; of Reginald Farrer, of Kingdon-Ward, of Chinese Wilson, of David Douglas, of many other people, a long list of people who were interested in plants, not the garden, for the two meet only in secret and in people as ordinary as me. And when thinking of this array of people, I remembered again that many of them did not die in their own beds: Douglas fell down a bear pit in Hawaii, Wilson died in a traffic accident in Boston after surviving seeing *Lilium regale* in its natural place, a riverbed in China; Farrer died of diphtheria in Burma. I shall die in a nursery.

PLANT HUNTING IN CHINA

Laura Lu asked, "Frank, do you want some water?" Frank did not want any water and Laura Lu said, "Frank, you don't want no water; y'all back there want some water?" We all back in the bus did not want any water, and Laura Lu said, "Y'all don't want any water, I guess I'll just drink all this water here all by myself. Y'all see that bird out there, that pretty little thing," but the bus was moving much too fast and so we did not see the bird, and Laura Lu said, "Y'all missed seeing that pretty little bird, I am telling you that was the prettiest little bird I ever see. This all so pretty, I'm so glad I came on this trip. When Frank came back last time he told me how beautiful this place was and he was right, it's so beautiful, it's so beautiful." Pierre said, "You would think they would . . ." and he made some scathing but perfectly accurate observation about the inef-

ficient or unsanitary way the people outside our bus were conducting
their lives; John said, "Come on, come on, let's go, everybody, let's get
going here." John had a voice that was not pleasing to anybody I knew,
and on top of that, he used it to excess. Dan sat in a corner at the back
of the bus and made jokes and cleaned the seeds he had just collected
with a not-ordinary intensity; Dan was afraid of the dangerous driving
on the dangerous roads in Yunnan Province, China, and he contained
his fears in this way—cleaning his seeds. George, a Swiss man who
works for the German seed company Jelito, had big teeth which could
be seen when he made his big smile, he had a big smile. Hans, who
works for a nursery in the Midwest specializing in plants that grow
particularly well in the shade, was tall and thin and pale and had big
teeth but not a mouth as big as George's, and laughed often but not
inappropriately. Grace, a woman, the owner of a nursery in Oregon,
was silent or did not speak so much; but when John had left our group
to go off and join another group, who were going to walk all over
Nepal, Grace said to me, "Well, now that John has gone, who do you
think is the leading candidate for asshole?" Grace laughed, I laughed,
I said, "Me," and Grace laughed again and turned away. I did not laugh
again, I stayed still. A few days before he left, John had called me a
bitch, though what he really said was that I was always bitchin', but I
decided that what he really meant was that I was a bitch, because
bitchin' can't be done by someone who isn't a bitch, or so it seems to
me. On the bus I sat way in the back between Ozzie and Dan. Ozzie
cleaned his seeds in a way that was exactly the opposite of Dan's:
slowly, almost tortoise-like, and this made Ozzie seem thoughtful.
Once, when we had gone into a restaurant to have our delicious dinner of pork, pork, pork, no fish, yak, vegetables, rice, and beer, we met

a woman singing. Her voice was not familiar to us and we all shrank from it, hoping we would be seated in a part of the restaurant far away from her. John said, "Isn't her voice horrible, doesn't the sound of it just drive you crazy?" And Ozzie said, very quietly, certainly not loud enough for anyone in particular to hear, "Little does he know, his voice has a similar effect." Paul, our group leader, a botanist and gardener with the Sarah Duke Gardens in North Carolina, a fervent Christian, wore a small gold cross on the tip of the collar of his shirt at all times. When I thought of the trouble he had to go through remembering to remove the cross from his dirty shirts and then to putting it back on his clean shirts, I became frightened of him; I am not a Christian, but I know all the same how fierce Christians can be toward people who do not feel the way they do; I never told Paul that I was afraid of him, and as far as I can remember, he never did anything, apart from wearing the cross on his shirt collar, to confirm my fear.

A journey like this, for someone like me, begins in so many ways: in a book by the plant hunter Frank Kingdon-Ward, *Plant Hunting on the Edge of the World,* an account of his travels looking for plants in China; a book by Ernest Wilson, *Plant Hunter's Paradise,* an account of his travels looking for plants in China; a book by Patrick Synge, *Mountains of the Moon,* an account of his travels looking for plants in Africa; a book by Reginald Farrer, *Among the Hills,* an account of his travels in the Alps looking for alpine plants; a repeated reading of the Heronswood catalogue from a nursery owned by the American plantsmen Dan Hinkley and Robert Jones; the journal that Meriwether Lewis and William Clark kept, an account of their travels to all that unmapped and unclaimed (by Europeans) land west of the Mississippi (they brought back all sorts of plant specimens to Thomas Jefferson);

walking out into my garden to deliberately feel and feel again the underside of the leaves of my *Rhododendron smirnowii* (it is native to the Caucasus)—all this is only a small part of how a journey like this, for someone like me, begins.

And what did I leave behind? Two children—a boy who is ten, a girl who is fourteen—a husband, a garden full of autumn color (hibiscus, aconitum, anemone, cimicifuga, crocus, maples, cercidiphyllum, franklinia, clematis, *Heptacodium miconioides*). And this was in front of me: Paul Jones (a director of the Sarah Duke Gardens in North Carolina), Frank and Laura Lu (two lawyers from North Carolina, married to each other), Ozzie Johnson (a landscape gardener and horticulturist from the Atlanta Botanical Gardens), George Ueberhart (a horticulturist with the Jelito seed company in Germany), Pierre Bunnerup (from Sunny Borders Nursery in Connecticut), Hans Hensen (from Shady Gardens in Missouri), John (just John), Guan Kaiyun (the director of Kunming Botanical Gardens in Kunming, China—he was our host and guide), Grace Dinsdale (the owner of Blooming Nurseries in Oregon, one of a very small number of women in America to own a nursery), Daniel J. Hinkley (Heronswood Nursery in Kingston, Washington), and an unknown landscape (unknown except for those books and the people who wrote them) of mountains and valleys and meadows full of plants (in seed) that I would like to grow in my garden, the garden I was leaving behind and which really needed my care. Everything I cared about needed me to care about it, but I went off anyway.

One morning I drove my children to the schoolbus stop, I got on an airplane that took me to Chicago, I took another airplane to Hong Kong, I took another airplane to Kunming, China. That first night (a

Sunday) I experienced the first of many doubts that the life I had left behind, life in a small village in Vermont, really existed, really was there and continued to be there in my absence. We were having a delicious dinner of Chinese food (though in China it is not Chinese food, it is only food) in a restaurant, and I went to the bathroom; it was not far away at all, it was right next to the kitchen, and on a table that was jammed up against a wall that separated kitchen and bathroom was a cauldron in which tea was brewed. As we were leaving the restaurant, I saw a large family having a wonderful time as they ate their dinner; it was so heartening it made me homesick, and I wanted to join them; but the baby of the family was having a bowel movement on the floor right then; it was all very comfortable for them, but I had come to China to collect seeds, not to be comfortable with what Chinese people did.

Dan (that is, Daniel Hinkley) and I were rooming together; I had requested it because he is my friend, the only person I knew on this expedition, and I felt very safe (he would like me no matter what) with him. This arrangement, of Dan and me, a man and a woman who were not married to each other, caused a small wave of disapproval; but Dan and I are both married—to other people, he to someone named Robert and I to someone named Allen, and we both had in common that we think of our marriages like breathing: ultimately fragile, so nothing must be done to compromise it. Looking back now, I can see what a pleasant, almost ideal couple we were: we never quarreled, we never caused each other any displeasure, we never longed to be rid of each other's presence. When I told my husband about Dan and me and how happy we were together and our lack of expressed irritation toward each other, he told me of that day's Ann Landers column: a woman had written to say that her husband was most attentive, giving her candy, bringing her flowers, considerate in every way you could imagine, but he had no interest in making love to her; what did it mean, she wanted to know. After Ann Landers printed this letter, she received over two hundred letters from other women requesting the name and address of this man.

The next day, a Monday, we were given a tour of Kunming Botanical Gardens by Guan (he had immediately become Guan to us, he wanted it that way), and it was my first time seeing the real botanists, as opposed to the nurserymen and -woman, in the grip of their passion. Ozzie, Paul, George, and Frank disappeared and Dan would have too, but I kept close to him. He was desperate to find seeds from the *Magnolia davidii,* but it had flowered many months ago and its fruit, which held the seeds, had long since fallen to the ground and rotted. He was much disappointed, but he pointed out to me things I had never even heard of: *Michelia maudii, Liriodendron sinensis* (I have planted and have thriving in my garden *Liriodendron tulipifera,* the species native to North America) and an evergreen witch hazel. The botanists were restless and frustrated by this little tour; none of them lived in the same zone as the Kunming Botanical Gardens, the plants growing there were not compelling to them.

That next day was really when the thing we had in mind began: collecting seeds. We were to go to Zhongdian and to stay for two days in Zhongdian collecting seeds from Hongshan Mountain; getting to Zhongdian would take two days and we would have to spend a night in the small city of Dali. It took a whole day in our minibus just to get there, and that first day the pattern of how we would spend the next four weeks was established; it was on that first day, too, that our personalities began to emerge, and by the time we got to the Red Camellia Hotel in Dali, we were all quite fixed. The botanists, all men, said the meanest things to each other in the nicest way, or the nicest things in the meanest way, and it was very funny, everybody laughed, and if I don't repeat them now, it's because when I told my husband what was said (and I told him what was said much later, after I had returned and everything was in the past), he looked puzzled and I

could see that it all had the quality of you-had-to-be-there. As they (the botanists) said these things to each other (mean and nice, nice and mean, all of it side-splittingly funny), their eyes were focused outside the bus, not so as to enjoy the scenery, which was increasingly beautiful in a way that I had never seen or imagined landscape to be, but to see if there were any places where they thought they might find something for their garden. They demanded a stop on what was a busy highway, they wanted to look around, but I suspect the truth was that, to them, sitting anywhere (a bus, a couch, a veranda) and looking at vegetation that might be in fruit was unbearable. The botanists and nurserymen and -woman all went off looking for things. They found nothing much on the way to Dali. I found a small flowering datura, unlike anything I had ever seen anywhere (in cultivation, or naturalized); it had small, perfect, trumpet-shaped white flowers and no fragrance (but it was the middle of the day and we were still in a tropical latitude). It was in fruit: fat pods with gently forbidding thorns. I gathered them, they are native to Mexico; how they made their way to China, I do not know.

On that first day we ate the food we would always eat. We stopped at a little restaurant for a delicious lunch of pork, pork, and pork (steamed, fried, congealed, and then sliced thinly), sautéed green leaves, sautéed bamboo, boiled rice, and beer. We got back on the bus and the botanists began their funny back-and-forth chatter, but their eyes were always glued to the landscape. After two and a half hours of sitting and looking, they demanded that a stop be made. They had seen an intriguing gulch in the side of a mountain; we were at a much higher elevation than Kunming, we were in an American zone 8, no longer in the tropics. They grabbed their collecting vests, their backpacks, their cameras, and rushed out of the bus. I followed Dan, not because I wished to collect anything (I live in an American zone 5) but because I wanted to get the feel of it, going up and down in this unfamiliar brush, looking and looking for some vegetable treasure with fruit on it; but I could not keep up with Dan; he bounded up the mountain like a four-footed furry mammal (a bear) and disappeared. I only knew how to follow him by seeing the trembly branches and flattened undergrowth that were left in his wake. I came upon a cow, which looked at me; I came upon a dog, which barked crossly at me. This surprised me; I had not expected to find a cross dog in China.

We got back to Dali and found the streets full of non-Chinese people, and I don't know if we looked as strange and out of place as they looked to me. We went out for a delicious dinner of pork, pork, pork, chicken, yak, sautéed vegetables, and beer, then went back to our rooms, slept, and the next morning, after a breakfast of rice noodles and instant coffee, got on the bus and started toward Zhongdian. We were climbing up now, higher and higher into the mountains, hairpin turn after hairpin turn, avoiding oncoming traffic as it avoided us; there were choruses of sharp intakes of breath, there were individual ahhhs; and the reason we were aware of each almost disastrous end is that we were looking out on an amazing landscape of hills, mountains, valleys, and terraces carved out of the mountains, cultivated, planted with corn—mostly corn, the rice grew in the valleys where we saw many people harvesting it—and as we drove through the villages that were in the mountains and the hills and the valleys, there was that strange, rotting, fetid, unpleasant smell of other people, their shit; human feces is such a valuable commodity in China, it is why all the vegetables were so vigorous-looking in cultivation, it is why people were so able to feed themselves. In all the time I was in China (four weeks spent in only two of its provinces) the thing I noticed people doing most frequently was growing food and eating food.

The botanists could take only so much sitting (three hours of driving); they demanded a stop. We had not reached the Yangtze, we were still among eucalyptus forests and bamboo, zone 8 or 7, but in the hills the botanists saw something. They collected seeds from arisaema, rhododendron (species not readily identifiable and so it became temporarily, until it bloomed, *Rhododendron sp.* or *spa*, as they jokingly pronounced it), hypericum, clematis, and other things which were new to me, but I could hear them speaking to each other in excitement about seeds from plants I had never seen or heard of in an American (or other) garden. I followed Dan, and this is how he got rid of me: he pointed to a cluster of red berries attached to a limp brown stem lying on the ground and said, "Here is your first ariseama." I was directed to my first real collection, my first distinguished collection, but after I had gathered the cluster of fruits, placing them in a Ziploc plastic bag (just the way Dan had instructed me), when I looked up again Dan was not there, he was way up above me, I could tell because he kept calling kindly to ask if I was all right. I was almost on the edge of the world (the world as I understood and do still understand it) and I was not all right; I wondered if Annie was all right, I wondered if Harold was all right; I took for granted that Allen was all right and loved me in the way he already loved me.

We drove along for miles and miles of seeing mountains and hills in front of mountains, and then the former mountains becoming mere hills and terraces carved out of the side of the hills (or mountains) planted with corn (or something else from that family), and then the road ran parallel to the Yangtze River and we could see places where the river had overflowed its normal barrier and destroyed crops of food and may have caused deaths. The Yangtze moved swift and furious, not like any river I had ever seen before (Mississippi, Missouri) but more like the sea, concentrated, boiled down, reduced. We drove over a bridge, crossing the Yangtze, and the botanists grew restless again; it had been four hours since the last stop; they had been seeing nothing but villages and the cultivation of plant life that goes with them (people settled, needing and tending a constant source of food); the Yangtze turned west or north (I know it turned away from us or we turned away from it), and we traveled along a road that paralleled one of its tributaries. For a very long time (or so it seemed to the botanists and to me, too—I was beginning to see things only from their point of view, I was beginning to see, even more pointedly, the landscape only from Dan's point of view), we saw nothing of interest, one-story building attached to rubber-coated wires (it was not the other way around), scrub and scrub and scrub (scrub as an entity holding nothing that the botanists thought of as garden-worthy, and that whole idea, "garden-worthy," will eventually have its own enemies, its own friends and passionate supporters), and then suddenly, meadow upon meadow of euphorbia growing wildly everywhere, starting at the road, going all the way up to a farmhouse, going beyond the farm to the foot of hills; turn after turn in the road would reveal this scene, meadows of euphorbia, the farmhouse, the euphorbia coming to a stop at the foot of hills; and then the landscape changed again, narrowing, and the mountains towered above us, and the sides of the mountains were covered with things even I could recognize: rodgersia (*pinnata,* it turned out), viburnum (*betulifolium,* it turned out), ligularia, astilbe (*chinensis,* it turned out), Rosa (*sericea pteracantha,* it turned out), impatiens, an evergreen dogwood (*Dendrobenthamia capitata*), *Clematis akebioidies,* a single climbing aconitum (*volubile,* it turned out); and all this just in a day's travel, from Dali to Zhongdian. It was dark when we arrived in Zhongdian; we washed, had a delicious dinner of pork, pork, pork, chicken, vegetables, no fish, rice, and beer, went back to our rooms to de-hiss and clean the seeds collected that day, went to bed just before midnight.

We all by then knew each other so well that it would not have been a surprise if some people had decided to spend the rest of a long life with one another, and it would not have been a surprise if some people never wanted to see one another again, even for a day. Laura Lu had the habit (charming sometimes, not charming sometimes) of asking you a question, repeating your answer, and then adding her response. It went like this: "Frank, you want some water? Frank, you don't want no water. I guess I'll just drink all this water myself." But it was consideration and affection for others that made her do this; when I was thirsty, I drank the bottled water we had with us and never asked anybody else if they wanted some. John (who shall have no other name, he is only John) had a voice that was not pleasant to the ears and he used it to excess. Hans, a very young plantsman, admired the older botanists, especially Dan. George, from Switzerland, was a plantsman with the German seed company Jelito. Grace, married for the second time, but only for three months, was missing her second husband. Pierre, a nurseryman for many years now, had the most interesting stories to tell, which were wonderful to hear each time he told them again and again. When observing groups of Chinese people do some perfectly monotonous thing that made the idea of work seem a curse and not an opportunity to explore the meaning of existence (and observing this chore being performed would make anyone understand the reason for automatization), Pierre would say, "Look at that, you would think they would have . . ." All his observations and statements were quite accurate, only he did not take note of the fact that our Chinese guides spoke English and may have thought his observations were criticisms. Ozzie was mostly quiet, tortoise-like looking at the landscape and tortoise-like gathering seeds from it, and often gathering the most desirable things. And Frank was married to Laura Lu.

I had by then had many of my nervous breakdowns (this is how I characterize my monumentally rude and truly insulting behavior—a temporary lapse in sanity). I found sitting down to a meal an experience filled with pleasure, the raised surface of my tongue swelling, shrinking, twisting, eventually simply surrendering (to xanthocarpom, which turned up frequently; in the weeks after I returned from China, I cooked Chinese food obsessively and could not find xanthocarpom and was not sorry); I found going to the lavatory so fraught with anxiety that I would not do it at all, except in cases where I had so cruelly controlled my natural bodily functions that they rebelled and forced me to do the necessary.

A week passed by after I left my family and I missed them and I missed my surroundings in Vermont; I was almost on the edge of the world (the world as I have come to know it); I could still speak to them directly through a telephone, but I was beginning to think that everything I had known, everyone I had known, was very far away and I might not be able to get back to them. One day later than a week, I felt sad, I felt sick, I stayed in bed, Dan said it was altitude sickness (we were in Zhongdian, a city miles and miles above sea level, enough to induce altitude sickness) and that may have been so, but I was, on the other hand, just about to have my menstrual period; I always take to my bed at that exact time. On the day I stayed in bed, the nursery people—Grace, Pierre, George, and Hans—went off to an alpine region while the botanists—Dan, Ozzie, Paul, and Frank—went off to another part of the mountain above Zhongdian. The nursery people got lost, the vehicle taking them up and then down collapsed on the way down, they had to walk for miles (which didn't bother Grace at all), they were very irritated that night at dinner. The botanists, on the other hand, had found many things they wanted, especially the

Meconopsis horridula (which I had never even heard of, other meconopsis yes, but *horridula*, no), and they were so pleased with themselves, pleased with their success; the botanists did utter some oh-ohs and ah-ahs of sympathy for the disappointment of the nursery people, but I was not at all convinced that they were sincere.

In Zhongdian, though, I noticed this about the botanists: wherever they found themselves, they looked forward to the next place: the place to come held the thing that was most desired, the place to come contained the satisfaction they longed for, the longing (for blooms, and blooms that were not normal to us), the emptiness (of blooms, blooms that were not in our normal surroundings), would be filled in the place to come. And so we went from Zhongdian to Deqen, but Deqen was not our real destination, Deqen was only a place to stay for three nights; it took two days on the bus to arrive at Deqen. On the way to Deqen we collected seeds of *Paeonia delavayi, Aconitum pendulicarpum,* philadelphus, thalictrum, and a maple (*Acer* something; Dan was not sure) on the side of a mountain just above Napa Hai. We were going to spend a night in a place called Benzilan. The botanists had been to Benzilan two years earlier and they had not liked it; they kept saying to me, each time I rudely whined about something (the toilet!), Just wait until you get to Benzilan. When we got to Benzilan both Grace (who never complained or said anything disagreeable) and I, without speaking to each other, immediately went to a store and bought aluminum pails in which to piss during the night. They were such handsome buckets; they cost about twenty-five cents each and I wished to bring them home even at the same time that I knew I never wanted to see them in any other situation besides the countryside of China again. That night after dinner (pork, pork, pork, no fish, the flesh of something that was a mammal other than pig, vegetables, rice, and beer) we sat on a balcony and drank beer and Scotch and watched a planet (Venus) come up and then stay still a little way above the ridge of mountains. We went to bed and awoke the next morning to the sounds of an animal being murdered for our breakfast and trucks taking on fuel and water. Benzilan was a town far from anywhere; it is a place where you stay on your way to somewhere else. I deeply loved Benzilan just for that, and in my mind all places of transition should be called that: Benzilan.

I was by then getting closer and closer to the edge of my world, that is to say, if the world as I had imagined it had a horizon beyond which I would fall and no longer know myself, I was then, in Benzilan, approaching it; after Benzilan I did not know myself, I could not speak to my family, I slept in a room with Dan (in separate beds), I saw Paul and Ozzie and Laura Lu and Hans and Frank and George and Pierre and Grace for breakfast and then again for dinner. When we got to Deqen, the evening of the morning after we left Benzilan, I came down with the monthly calamity that is my menstrual period and took to my bed for all of the following day. And so I began feeling the loss of my family and the comforts of every kind that I associate with them.

One morning (again, one morning!) coming down the stairs of the Duo-wen Hotel in Benzilan, I fell and sprained my ankle. Two days later, when collecting the seeds of a clematis not far from the Beimashan Pass, in excitement I turned too quickly and twisted the very same ankle. I fell, I cried out, no one answered me; I then followed the path along a fiercely rushing stream; I unexpectedly came upon Dan and Ozzie lying on their stomachs adoring a begonia they had longed to see in the wild and were now seeing in its natural habitat. On that same day (the day of respraining my ankle) Dan was certain that he had come upon *Rheum davidii* (a rhubarb with leaves the size of a half dollar), and he collected seeds from it and was happy for an hour or so, before deciding that he had not collected *Rheum davidii* at all but only a pesty polygonatum; he was much depressed by this, even though he already had this same rhubarb *davidii* growing in his garden; it had been given to him by that great gardener in Ireland Helen Dillon.

And after three days we left Deqen to go to Weixi, meaning to take a road that ran along the Mekong River and of course stopping along the way to collect seeds. Dan's friend Daryl, a specialist in epimedium, had told Dan of areas along this road where different species of this plant, epimedium, would be abundant; but one hour out of the city of Deqen, the road had collapsed (some of the mountain above had just rolled down onto the road), and so we had to retrace our path, going back to Deqen, back to Beimashan, back to Benzilan, back to Zhongdian. We went back the way we had come as if we had never seen it before, with enthusiasm, with happiness; we collected again, things we already had and things we had missed; we ate a delicious lunch of pork, pork, pork, pork, vegetables, rice, and beer in Benzilan, in a restaurant right next to the Duo-wen Hotel. We got back to Zhongdian way before dark, and Dan took a taxi to a place out of town so he could collect the seeds of a special birch; he had meant to collect it when we were first in Zhongdian, had forgotten then, and was very glad to have the chance to do it again; he had already collected and grown this plant in his nursery, but by mistake he had sold them all and had not kept any for his own garden.

We got to Weixi after a whole day of sitting on the bus, stopping only for lunch, delicious as usual and in just the way we had come to expect, and one stop for collecting (I collected a particularly large flowering St. Johns wort); in Weixi we bathed in the kind of bathrooms we were accustomed to (the kind of bathrooms I had become accustomed to), ate a delicious dinner of pork, pork, pork, pork, noodles, beef, vegetables, rice, and beer; I walked back to my room with my arm linked through Paul's; I saw a rat, screamed, and Paul did not make fun of me. My twice-sprained ankle had begun to look like an unusual garden implement: from my ankle to my toes was such a huge swelling that my calf looked unusually thin, as if it were the handle of the tool that was the rest of my foot. I bound it up with a bandage I had bought at Wal-Mart in Vermont, stamped *Made in China,* but I could not find any bandages like it in any of the stores I frequented in that part of China.

In Weixi I stayed in bed nursing my ankle, went to lunch with Pierre, walked around and met a woman selling coins that had been in circulation in Indochina in 1918; I bought one for about twenty-five American cents, I did not know if it was authentic and I did not really care. By that time in Weixi I had become used to walking around among ordinary Chinese people and causing a sensation; they had never seen a person with my complexion before; mothers and fathers would draw my presence to their children's attention and they were not discreet about it; I did not mind, I was in their country. I did not forget my own family then, but I did not miss them, nothing I saw reminded me of them, not the children, not the husbands, not the wives, not the houses, which do not have sloping roofs, not the market where I could buy a chicken whose neck had been just partially cut or an aphrodisiac made from the ground-up penis of a mammal. In the mountains near Weixi, Dan found a climbing Solomon's seal and some other plants, but everyone was very excited about the climbing Solomon's seal, and he immediately agreed to share his collection of its seeds.

That morning, just as we were getting on the bus to leave Weixi (it might have been a Wednesday, it might have been a Thursday, it might have been a Friday, none of us knew the names of the days anymore, only that it was day and then it was night), there was a huge commotion in the courtyard near the kitchen; something (mammal) was screaming in agony, the pathetic, last, hopeless appeal that mammals make before they die (and they know it well, for so much of the time they are the cause of it). Among us there were many oh Gods and oh Christs and oh shits; but Hans and I went to see what or who was making such a cry. This is what we saw: a very big pig, its two front legs tied together, its two back legs tied together, surrounded by four people; one of them held the pig's head, another one was plunging a knife into its neck; the pig's cries grew louder and then softer, blood spurted out of its neck, and someone held a large basin in place to catch the blood; the basin quickly filled up with blood, it was too small to hold all the pig's blood. Hans and I joined the rest of our group on the bus. This incident was never mentioned again. For lunch we ate our delicious meal of pig, pig, pig, pig, pig, no fish, many vegetables cooked in fat rendered from pig, rice, and beer; that evening in Judian, we ate our delicious dinner of pork, pork, pork, pork, pork, no fish, many vegetables sautéed in fat rendered from the flesh of a pig, rice, and beer.

It was in Judian that I had my most serious nervous breakdown. I went to our Chinese guide and said this: "The rooms are the filthiest rooms I have ever been in; there is blood on the walls, there is shit on the walls, there are the remains of vomit on the walls." Judian was the place where our guide had been born and grew up; but I did not know this when I spoke those words, I only knew because Paul gave me a lecture on other people's reality, on other people's feelings, and though he did not mention that dreaded word "acceptance" he implied that I should accept the things I was faced with. I did not think, What a Christian! then, I only wished I had thought it then, so I could regret my prejudice now. And it was John who said to me that our experience was more authentic the closer we came to the Chinese, and by that he meant the major and minor stooping situation that I had been complaining about; he said that the whole experience of the unsanitariness of everything, the preparation of our food, the places in which we ate and slept (all this according to my feelings, not my scientific evidence, I have no scientific evidence, I don't even believe in such a thing as scientific evidence), that all of this made our experience in China more authentic. And I thought to myself, Well, the last time I had such an intimate experience with anybody was with my children, changing their diapers, cleaning up their vomit when they had a flu, cooking their food, and worrying about where it, their food, came from (strawberries from Chile or California), and I do not think all of that makes our relationship more authentic, I could have done without all of it, the vomit, the blood, the shit; I only said all this to myself, I did not say any of this to anybody, not to John; I did not say to John, I like the Chinese, I like the way they grow food (I would then be thinking of how those terraces and terraces were cultivated), I like the way they eat food, it is the things they do in between growing and eating I don't like, the things they do after eating the food, I don't understand that; all the things I thought, everything I thought, I did not say one word of to John. I only looked at him (John); he caressed his beard (he had a beard), he stroked his nose between his thumb and his forefinger as if to refine it (his nose); and all this about John—caressing his beard, stroking his nose, the sound of his voice, his opinions on authenticity or inauthenticity—made me sorry for the people who would be on a hike with him in Nepal (this was to come), made me sorry for people who would not or could not speak freely (to him, a simple man, or to something more complicated than a simple man); but just as I was having feelings of sympathy for John and all who would meet or could meet John, it was then that he said (John did) I was always bitchin' and bitchin', and it was then that I transformed him saying this ("bitchin' and bitchin'") into him actually calling me a bitch, and at that moment he was ashamed of himself for using those words ("bitchin' and bitchin' ") and I was suddenly glad that I had bitched and bitched. If a person who stroked his beard and caressed his nose was against bitching, then most certainly a person like me must be a bitch. When John said that I had been "bitchin' and bitchin' " and I had then turned this phrase into a badge of honor for myself, he had not expected that, he was cowed, he was quiet after that, we parted with heartfelt kisses, and only time will tell if those heartfelt kisses were forever. If I were to see him again I would be so pleased, especially if he did go off to build those houses for Habitat for Humanity; he talked a great deal about that during the time I felt him to be unendurable, and that and that alone mitigated my desire to slice his head off his body. Even now (especially now), I am glad an impulse for good (building homes for people who had none) intervened between my desire for something bad and my desire for something that was not bad. I did not like John; I did not hate John, I only did not like him, and when he was gone (off to walk on a trail that ran among the foothills of the Himalayan Mountains, and I was very envious of that, even though I had never imagined such a thing until John mentioned it) I missed him.

And by that time again, I was so far away from everything that had come to have meaning for me (my children, my husband, the home in which I lived, the other people I saw every day), that the world I knew only through the telephone or through some other form of communication receded and receded and I could barely remember it, and was uncertain that I would see it again. Driving along the Yangtze River as it went one way, and then driving along the Yangtze as it went in an opposite direction, taking a dramatic (to me, at any rate) turn; driving toward the Mekong and then the road disappearing; driving along a road that had been cut out in the middle of a formidable ridge (a mountain), the whole thing reduced to something a child would construct out of sand on a beach, if a child was granted such a luxury. The botanists, their eyes searching the sides of the mountains for areas beyond which they could just sense lay a rich collection of plants that had set seed, would demand a stop, and then another; they were so voracious, but only for plants that had set fruit; they did not eat an enormous amount of food, they all lost much of their evidence of American physical prosperity (fat) after three weeks; they stopped and stopped and collected and collected; once we had to stop because two vehicles going in opposite directions had collided while going around a blind bend; no one was hurt, but it took a while to clear the road; it was there one botanist collected *Iris colettii,* a species of iris I had never heard of before.

To see Dali again was reassuring and all those strange people (natives of Denmark, France, England, the Netherlands); their presence no longer annoyed me, I was only curious about them, my curiosity did not need to be satisfied. At that time there was a big moon in the sky, a full moon; and to see such a thing as that moon, so familiar, and those people (from Denmark, France, England, the Netherlands), so familiar, made me feel confident, made me feel as if the world would be mine again, I could dismiss the things I did not like (the certainty of the people from Denmark, France, England, the Netherlands); and so when I saw a funeral, someone being buried in a city in China, I was curious, I wondered what that was like, to miss someone forever in a place like that, Dali, China. Some of the mourners had wrapped their heads in white cloth, some of the mourners carried an old framed picture of the dead person, some of the mourners wept, some of the mourners held the weepers in their arms, some of the mourners took turns carrying the coffin, some of the mourners banged on drums and some played tunes on a reed instrument. The coffin was painted red and was shiny, as if freshly lacquered; I was sorry, just at that moment, that I did not know the person inside it, and I was glad, just then, I did not know the person inside it; to be sorry, gladness should come first, but when sorrow comes, I can never remember that I had once been glad. It went through Dali, the entire procession, some weeping (the people walking behind the coffin), some laughing (the people who took turns carrying the coffin), and when they got to a part in their travels that separated Dali from the burial grounds, the people carrying the coffin ran away from the rest of the mourners; the rest of the mourners seemed devastated, the rest of the mourners pretended to be devastated (this is how it seemed to me), and then there was the loud noise of firecrackers and the smell of things burning (but not seriously burning), and then the mourners carrying the coffin proceeded up a long, steep hill; the other mourners, the ones left behind, looked longingly at the disappearing people carrying the coffin.

But it was the familiarity of Dali (the funeral reminding me of death, the bars where I could buy whiskey and rum and vodka, the restaurants where I could buy coffee or something resembling coffee, a hamburger, a toilet where my bodily remains disappeared when I pressed a lever, people who took a tip as a reward for their satisfactory service) that made me miss my husband, my children, my home, my garden with everything in it dying, going dormant. The botanists and their companions (the nursery people) went off to a place called

Huadianba, to search for something that would make the American garden (a luxury) even more beautiful, but my ankle (which looked more than ever like a serviceable implement in the history of the American garden) hindered me from joining them. They came back in a rush, they came back excited, they came back with tales of not enough beer, too much solitude, not enough seeds from plants they expected to find in seed; they came back saying how wonderful everything had been, they came back looking forward to going to Emeishan. Between Dali and Emeishan we stopped in Kunming (again) and Chengdu. Kunming and then Dali seemed like Paris (the capital of France, not the plant the botanist had been seeking); and then, long after, Kunming and Chengdu seemed like themselves, not like anything I had known before, not like anything I wanted to know again, like places (cities) in my imagination, like places (cities) I had heard or read about. In Kunming we ate pork, pork, pork, beef (not yak), fish, vegetables, rice, and beer; we sent by special post to North America all the seeds we had collected in Yunnan Province. John left for his trek in the Himalayas, a woman named Elsa replaced him; it was then, when John had left, that Grace asked me who would take his place as asshole and I said that I would, though I was not happy to take his place. Elsa and Grace were assigned to room with each other. Grace liked Elsa very much, we all liked Elsa very much, Elsa was so very nice, we all missed John so very much, we had come to like John very much.

We flew to Chengdu (the capital of Szechuan Province), and then took a bus to the foothills of Emeishan, a mountain holy to people of the Buddhist faith. There are places on this earth to which you are drawn because they promise to make you forget where you are from, and there are other places, existing all by themselves, and they make you forget where you are from and where you were just the other day. Emeishan was such a place. It had a history: a holy mountain, one of the most holy mountains to Buddhism; it was so holy that hundreds of years ago steps were built that led from its base to its summit, so that people could walk up (to see Nirvana, the place, or just simply the state of mind) or down (at which point they perhaps might come to the realization that Nirvana is neither a place nor a state of mind).

At the base of Emeishan, the botanists collected the seeds of a begonia, a hepatica, an epimedium with leaves twice the size of my palm and shiny as if they had been polished by a very industrious person. It takes three days or so for a devoted pilgrim to walk up to the summit of Emeishan; it took us a day to walk almost three-quarters of this same path down the mountain. Walking down, I collected the seeds of *Astilbe grandis, Viburnum nervosa, Buddleia forrestii,* and *Aconitum volubile* (a climbing monkshood); and when walking down those stairs, I once again wondered where I was, where I really was, and if I would find my way home again, if I would ever see the things that were most familiar, the things that I most loved, again: my children, my husband, my friends, the garden; the garden I have made and loved was in back of me, the garden I hoped to have and so hoped to love was in front of me, at my feet, on the slopes of this mountain that was holy to some people, not to me. It was on this mountain that we came across bands of monkeys, native to that part of the world, native to that mountain, and they were very unpleasant, reminding me of myself, my relatives, people I might actually know: they were beautiful, they were demanding, they were greedy, they were ill-mannered, they were violent; they jumped on the back of a woman from France and ripped her knapsack apart in a flash, they tore off a pocket on someone else's jacket; when I saw a band of them approaching me, hissing and baring their teeth, I screamed and pushed in front of me a young woman named Jen, a young woman half as old as I. She only realized I was serious about using her as a shield when she found my fingernails burrowing into the soft flesh of her arm. Jen staved the monkeys off for me and Hans, too, and after that I walked down the stairs confidently, because I asked everyone I met coming up if there were any monkeys below, and they always said no; and I believed them, even though I wasn't sure they understood me, for they were all Chinese, and they remained so, stubbornly . . . Chinese. I walked and walked all day, stopping only for a delicious lunch of pork, pork, pork, noodles, eggs, tomatoes, and rice at a wayside restaurant; I ate that meal with Dan and Ozzie and Hans and Laura Lu and Frank; near the end of the day, with my destination not more than a quarter of a mile away (I could even see the end of the walk, a sharp drop of stairs below me), I could not walk anymore. I could not feel my own legs, they would not do what I commanded them to do, and I started to cry. Dan came upon me going down the stairs on my bottom, like a baby just learning the mechanics of walking, and he tried to carry me in his arms, but to take his mind off what a burden I was to him, he told jokes and made me laugh so much that I became more of a burden laughing than I had been when I was crying. I then paid two men three hundred yuan to carry me to the end of the trail; they had charged me sixty, but I was so grateful to them for carrying me one quarter of a mile or so that I would have given them more than was required.

When coming down Emeishan, Grace wandered off the path to get a better view and she almost fell off a ridge into nothing for hundreds of feet before the nothing changed into naked rocks; when she told us of this experience, we were all shaken, and the next day she went off to Shanghai to make contact with people who propagate tree peonies, and after she left we all would say to each other, from time to time, "I wonder how Grace is doing," for Grace had left us and took her spontaneity, her impetuosity, all amounting to a kind of loneliness; we never heard from her again and I missed her, especially at the last meal we all ate together; the botanists and I wanted to have our serving of rice at the same time we had our delicious servings of pork, pork, pork, pork, yak, vegetables sautéed in pork renderings, chicken, and no fish, not after; we gestured, we spoke loudly, we gestured, we spoke loudly, but nothing we said or did conveyed any meaning to our waitress. Ozzie then got up and went into the kitchen and showed the waitress the pot of rice, and that was how we got to eat rice at the same time as our other food. It was then Pierre said, "Isn't this funny? We want rice, the place is full of rice, but we don't know how to ask for rice; you would think by now we could have figured out how to say 'rice' in Chinese." It was then I missed Grace, and that was also the last time I missed Grace.

We said goodbye to each other in Hong Kong. I had collected the seeds of 130 different flowering plants. I would send them to Andrew and to Jack, two men who grow many things from seed for me. I got on a plane early one morning and I flew through that morning and a night, and then arrived in Chicago on the very same morning that I left Hong Kong. All that I left behind was real enough: the days on the bus in the company of the same people, wearing the same clothes (I loved their smells); the same food—pork, pork, pork, rice, vegetables, yak, fish every once in a while, I never grew sick of it; Benzilan, where the

moon looked strange in the sky and the sky itself looked not real, or not like the sky I had gotten to know; the glacier I could see at Beimashan Pass, a glacier in a place that on the map is at the same latitude as Cuba; the toilets that did not work—the toilets will never work, they have a different idea altogether about hygiene; my grumpiness, my bitchiness, my nervous breakdowns; the wet meadows of primulas; the gulleys filled with columbine and meadow rue and sanguisorba chewed to the ground by grazing yaks; the grazing yaks themselves; walking hurriedly to meet the bus and coming upon a large colony of *Primula capitata* in seed; the rhododendrons and the rhododendrons and the rhododendrons again—so many different species would have to bloom before even Dan could say with certainty what they are; all those people who stared at me, all those people I would have stared at if I had seen just one of them in my small village in Vermont. I slipped back into my life of mom, sweetie, and the garden; I was given much help by buying a fashion magazine that had on its cover a picture of that all-powerful and keenly discerning literary critic Oprah Winfrey.

THE GARDEN
I HAVE IN MIND

I know gardeners well (or at least I think I do, for I am a gardener, too, but I experience gardening as an act of utter futility). I know their fickleness, I know their weakness for wanting in their own gardens the thing they have never seen before, or never possessed before, or saw in a garden (their friends'), something which they do not have and would like to have (though what they really like and envy—and especially that, envy—is the entire garden they are seeing, but as a disguise they focus on just one thing: the Mexican poppies, the giant butter burr, the extremely plump blooms of white, purple, black, pink, green, or the hellebores emerging from the cold, damp, and brown earth).

I would not be surprised if every gardener I asked had something definite that he or she liked or envied. Gardeners always have some-

thing they like intensely and in particular, right at the moment you
engage them in the reality of the borders they cultivate, the space in
the garden they occupy; at any moment, they like in particular this, or
they like in particular that, nothing in front of them (that is, in the borders they cultivate, the space in the garden they occupy) is repulsive

and fills them with hatred, or this thing would not be in front of them. They only love, and they only love in the moment; when the moment has passed, they love the memory of the moment, they love the memory of that particular plant or that particular bloom, but the plant of the bloom itself they have moved on from, they have left it behind for something else, something new, especially something from far away, and from so far away, a place where they will never live (occupy, cultivate; the Himalayas, just for an example).

Of all the benefits that come from having endured childhood (for it is something to which we must submit, no matter how beautiful we find it, no matter how enjoyable it has been), certainly among them will be the garden and the desire to be involved with gardening. A gardener's grandmother will have grown such and such a rose, and the smell of that rose at dusk (for flowers always seem to be most fragrant at the end of the day, as if that, smelling, was the last thing to do before going to sleep), when the gardener was a child and walking in the grandmother's footsteps as she went about her business in her garden—the memory of that smell of the rose combined with the memory of that smell of the grandmother's skirt will forever inform and influence the life of the gardener, inside or outside the garden itself. And so in a conversation with such a person (a gardener), a sentence, a thought that goes something like this—"You know, when I was such and such an age, I went to the market for a reason that is no longer of any particular interest to me, but it was there I saw for the first time something that I have never and can never forget"—floats out into the clear air, and the person from whom these words or this thought emanates is standing in front of you all bare and trembly, full of feeling, full of memory. Memory is a gardener's real palette; memory as it summons up the past, memory as it shapes the present, memory as it dictates the future.

I have never been able to grow *Meconopsis betonicifolia* with success (it sits there, a green rosette of leaves looking at me, with no bloom. I look back at it myself, without a pleasing countenance), but the picture of it that I have in my mind, a picture made up of memory (I saw it some time ago), a picture made up of "to come" (the future, which is the opposite of remembering), is so intense that whatever happens between me and this plant will never satisfy the picture I have of it (the past remembered, the past to come). I first saw it (*Meconopsis betonicifolia*) in Wayne Winterrowd's garden (a garden he shares with that other garden eminence Joe Eck), and I shall never see this plant (in flower or not, in the wild or cultivated) again without thinking of him (of them, really—he and Joe Eck) and saying to myself, It shall never look quite like this (the way I saw it in their garden), for in their garden it was itself and beyond comparison (whatever that amounts to right now, whatever that might ultimately turn out to be), and I will always want it to look that way, growing comfortably in the mountains of Vermont, so far away from the place to which it is endemic, so far away from the place in which it was natural, unnoticed, and so going about its own peculiar ways of perpetuating itself (perennial, biannual, monocarpic, or not).

I first came to the garden with practicality in mind, a real beginning that would lead to a real end: where to get this, how to grow that. Where to get this was always nearby, a nursery was never too far away; how to grow that led me to acquire volume upon volume, books all with the same advice (likes shade, does not tolerate lime, needs staking), but in the end I came to know how to grow the things I like to grow through looking—at other people's gardens. I imagine they acquired knowledge of such things in much the same way—looking and looking at somebody else's garden.

But we who covet our neighbor's garden must finally return to our own, with all its ups and downs, its disappointments, its rewards. We come to it with a blindness, plus a jumble of feelings that mere language (as far as I can see) seems inadequate to express, to define an attachment that is so ordinary: a plant loved especially for something endemic to it (it cannot help its situation: it loves the wet, it loves the dry, it reminds the person seeing it of a wave or a waterfall or some event that contains so personal an experience as when my mother would not allow me to do something I particularly wanted to do and in my misery I noticed that the frangipani tree was in bloom).

I shall never have the garden I have in my mind, but that for me is the joy of it; certain things can never be realized and so all the more reason to attempt them. A garden, no matter how good it is, must never completely satisfy. The world as we know it, after all, began in a very good garden, a completely satisfying garden—Paradise—but after a while the owner and the occupants wanted more.

THE GARDEN IN EDEN

The narrative of the garden that I know begins in Eden, the Garden of Eden, and this garden, Eden, comes at the very end of creation, after Adam, before Eve, because she comes as a companion for Adam, not endemic to the garden at all, just as a companion for Adam as he enjoys the garden, and so it is so shocking that her presence itself leads to his being deprived of his enjoyment (I was having this thought one day in late September 1998, while walking on a winding, dusty road in Yunnan Province, China). And in this narrative with which I am familiar, this place called Eden is an ideal as a state of mind and an ideal as a place in which to live day after day after day; and Eden, in this text with which I am familiar, begins with pleasure and necessity, but then again the Tree of Life (which I think of as the vegetable garden, a need) comes before the

Tree of Knowledge (which I think of as the plants for which I have no immediate use and grow only for an interest that is peculiar to me, and so this is the part of the garden which carries me into the world). In any case, Eden is tilled and generally looked after so that it can yield physical nourishment before it becomes a danger to Adam's inner life. This is the garden! I said to myself, as I walked up and down the side of some mountains in southwestern China, this is the garden! I was thinking of the beginning of so many garden books I have read, I was thinking of the accounts of gardens by the many gardeners I have read, and I was thinking, Is this Eden, that thing that was banished, turned out into the world as I have come to know it—the world of discarding only to reclaim, of rejecting and then claiming again, the world of such longing that its end (death) is a relief?

But I was in southwestern China, walking up and down mountains, walking into forests of mostly rhododendrons, and then sometimes a small crop of paris or hydrangeas or enkianthus or maples or, coming out of the forest, on the edge of it, finding some apples or something so unfamiliar I would have to call Ron Pembroke (he is the person who removes or places trees in my part of Vermont) to remove things that looked to me like weeds.

The rhododendrons did not seem like weeds, but perhaps that was because they were familiar, I had paid money for the *Rhododendron smirnowii*, which is similar in leaf to the ones now before me (in China), each leaf covered with soft felt (indumentum) underneath, making the leaf appear silvery from afar or making the leaf seem puzzling (in a garden way) from afar. The irises, grassy-looking and growing thickly together, matted and tangled, also did not seem like a weed; and there were primroses and gentians and thalictrum and columbine (*Aquilegia rockii*) and all kinds of impatiens that I had never seen or heard of before, and rodgersia and ligularia (not exactly the ones I had been growing, I had been growing and had been exposed only to cultivars), and everything before me was familiar just the way I was seeing it (the primulas, the iris, the rodgersia) or in the form of a cultivar (the ligularia), and I had this not original thought that everything I saw before me was in a state of banishment, as was I (for I at that moment was without my family, my two children, my husband, the large house we had made habitable for ourselves), and so I thought (again) of the garden I had left at home, which was orderly, or meant to be orderly, and then I was reminded of the garden Eden, the garden to which all gardens must refer, whether they want to or not.

What turned wrong with Eden (from my point of view) is so familiar: the owner grew tired of the rigid upkeep of His creation (and I say His on purpose), of the rules that could guarantee its continued perfect existence, and most definitely tired of that design of the particular specimen (Tree of Life, Tree of Knowledge) as the focal point in the center and the other configurations (alleys, parterres, orchards, potageries; the cottage garden, which is really an illustration of making the best of deep social injustice, as the ha-ha, a part of the gardening landscape, is an illustration of making something beautiful out of yet another social cruelty. And the caretakers, the occupants (Adam and then Eve), too, seemed to have grown tired of the demands of the Gardener and most certainly of His ideas of what the garden ought to be, not so much how it ought to be arranged but whether its layout ought to remain intact, for this layout became boring to them after a while, this layout was not theirs, this layout (the Tree of Knowledge and the Tree of Life at its center) had all the sadness that comes with satisfaction.

But gardeners (the owners of gardens, the occupants of them, which is to say, the people who work in them) are so restless, so irritable, so constantly vexed, so happy with their unhappiness, so pleased that they cannot really be satisfied; I can see how that narrative (the original one of Eden) would end and then evolve. Gardeners quarrel in their hearts loudly, vow to be without forgiveness, and then cannot help but share their just-found seedlings, clones, and favorable plots. It is so with the original gardener (I was thinking this while tramping around and over hill and dale and climbing up mountains and crossing furiously rushing streams): possessive, generous, temperamental, steadfast, single-minded, patient, quick to toss out, easy to make smile, slow to anger and then quick to anger, quick to make resolutions and then quick to break them. That gardener, any gardener, is not a stable being; that gardener, any gardener, is not a model of consistency. I was thinking all this in China, in the part of China, southwest Yunnan, in places called Napa Hai, Zhongdian, Deqen, Weixi, on the way to Beimashan, on the way to Emeishan, in Chengdu, in Kunming.

For all the years I had been a gardener, any rhododendron with felted leaves seemed so exotic (coming from far away, unfamiliar, rare, hard to come by—this is my own definition) and expensive, it always costs so much more; I can remember the time I first came across such a thing, a rhododendron with indumentum; it was in Mr. Carlson's garden in Salem, New York. Mr. Carlson was a plantsman who specialized in rhododendrons and so he had many kinds, and just as I was leaving, just about to get into my car, he showed me some of his yak rhododendrons, and he very offhandedly showed me the felt on the underside of their leaves, and how surprised I was to see this and how pleased he was by my surprise and how pleased he looked when I wanted to buy some of these plants and he had none to sell to me. Mr. Carlson was such a nice man, and how sad it makes me to say that after that day I have never bought a thing from him, though he still sends me his catalogue. (I was thinking all this in China, in those places I have mentioned before, those places I will never forget so long as I am in the garden, so let me just mention them again: Napa Hai, Deqen, Weixi). And in China, as I walked up and down and across, I was often lost in forests of rhododendrons, and their leaves on the underside were covered with that substance, indumentum, and it was not rare, the indumentum, all the rhododendrons' leaves were like that.

There have been so many times since I have become a gardener that I have brought my family to the brink of bankruptcy just to have growing in my garden some treasure (to me) or another, something I felt I could not live happily in the garden without; I could not live without the rhododendron 'Jane Grant' and the rhododendron 'Anna H. Hall'; *R.* 'Jane Grant' in particular costs a lot, she is available only through the White Flower Farm nursery, but she (and I mean that, she) is very beautiful, for *R. yakushimanum,* the species with its felted leaves, is a part of her ancestry; *R.* 'Anna H. Hall,' also a descendant of *R. yak,* is not as rare, but it is costly anyway. *R. smirnowii* I bought from Dan; they were only six inches tall when I bought them. And when I was in China (in all those places with those names) in the forests with the rhododendrons of the felted leaves, I wondered (again, for I had thought of this many times before, even as I have thought of it many times since) if I was in the original garden (or a part of it, always a part of it), Eden, or something like it, only this time turned inside out, only this time (in China) the garden was in a state of banishment; I was in the wild, the garden had become the wild and I was in it (even though all the time I was really in China). I tried to bring everything back in, for I had (have) come to see that a garden, to make a garden, is partly an attempt to do that, to bring in from the wild as many things as can be appreciated, as many things as it is possible for a gardener to give meaning to, as many things as it is possible for the gardener to understand.

One day I was walking around in a very large garden in England, and this garden took up acres and acres of land and it was divided into many sections, the evergreen plants were in one place, the plants native to bare, high mountains were in one place, and then a whole enormous section of the garden was made to look like (or said to look like) a Himalayan glade. I do not now know a glade in the Himalayas, I have never been to the Himalayas; but whoever made this garden had an idea of it from actually having been there or had seen a picture of it. What would be in a real glade in the real Himalayas? What would such a thing look like? In that garden in England there were acres and acres devoted to rhododendrons, and rocks, huge bare rocks, and perhaps other things. When I saw the Himalayan glade in England, the rhododendrons were not in bloom, and if I had not known that it was meant to re-create a part of the landscape that makes up an uncultivated part of the surface of the earth that is the Himalayan Mountains, I would not have known what I was looking at, I would have thought that I was in an unkept part of this large estate. I walked around this part of the Himalayan glade for a long time, going over and over the same area, and then I was exhausted; I walked around the sides of mountains in China, never going over the same area twice, and then I was exhausted. In the Himalayan glade, in the mountains in China, both times I went home and, after eating a delicious supper, went to bed.

What exactly is the wild garden, then? I said these words to myself, once when I was sitting in a room; in this room are many books about the garden and one of these books is William Robinson's *The Wild Garden.* I have seen his garden at Gravetye (in England, and on the very same day that I saw the attempt to re-create the Himalayan glade) and it is an arrangement of things carefully attended to, so that it (the garden at Gravetye) looks neglected, abandoned. What exactly is the wild garden, then?—and as I said these words to myself, as I asked myself this question, I was sitting in this room with many books about the garden, but I was not idle altogether, I was trying, with no success, to remove some randomly growing hairs from my chin (a sign of my age, I have noticed that old women have randomly placed strands of hair growing on their chins) and I was tugging at them just the way I would if they were weeds (I only think of this now, for I am tugging at them at this very minute). William Robinson said this in 1870 (*The Wild Garden*): "It has nothing to do with the idea of the 'Wilderness.' It does not mean the picturesque garden, for a garden may be highly picturesque, and yet in every part the result of ceaseless care." And here again: "Some have thought of it as a garden run wild, or sowing annuals in a muddle; whereas it does not interfere with the regulation flower garden at all . . . I wish it to be kept distinct in the mind from the various sorts of hardy plant cultivation in groups, beds, and borders, in which good gardening and good taste may produce many happy effects." And while this idea of the "Wild Garden" was very clear to William Robinson, the luxury of stating and enjoying the results of your own will, your own idea of how the things in front of you ought to be, to do what a God would do! But gods are so likely always to feel themselves so very misunderstood, for by the time a new edition of his book was issued in 1894, he said this in a new foreword: "Many of the reviewers of this book did not take the trouble necessary to see its true motive, and some of them confuse it with the picturesque garden, which may be formed in many costly ways, whereas the idea of the wild garden is placing plants of other countries, as hardy as our hardiest wild flowers, in places where they will flourish without further care or costs."

And his idea of the Wild Garden is so interesting, for all the plants he lists that ought to be in it are ones that are very commonplace now. I mean, even I am familiar with them, and it is true that none of them, as far as I can tell, are native to Great Britain. In a chapter headed "Hardy Exotic Flowering Plants," he lists sedum, marsh mallow, thalictrum, daylily, hens and chicks among many others; and almost everything mentioned I now know well, I now know some of them so well, I consider them a nuisance (the daylily) and often regret that I ever loved them in the first place.

And so again to Eden, and again to the sides of the mountains in Yunnan and Szechuan Provinces, China, and again to the Wild Garden and to the Himalayan glade. What does a gardener want? A gardener wants the garden to behave in the way she says, and when it does not, she will turn it out, abandon it, she will denounce the garden, not in general, only as it is particular to her, and we who come after will have to take some of what she loved and some of what she didn't love, and accept that there are some things we cannot take because we just don't understand them. The Himalayan glade seemed a parch, dusty wilderness to me; when I saw Gravetye, it was an Eden I loved so much, one from which I could not wait to escape. Gravetye is now an ideal luxurious inn; I had a delicious lunch in the dining room, and while eating I was struck with the desire to behead all of my fellow diners who were not traveling with me (Jill and Aunt Annie) because . . . because . . . because. Eden is like that, so rich in comfort, it tempts me to cause discomfort; I am in a state of constant discomfort and I like this state so much I would like to share it.